# Pinpoints of Light

## Escaping the Abyss of Abuse

Dear Reader,

There is always hope!

Show up Shining

♥ April Giauque

### APRIL T GIAUQUE

Pinpoints of Light

Copyright © 2018 April Giauque

Printed in the United States of America

Published by Author Academy Elite

P.O. Box 43, Powell, OH 43035

Paperback: 978-1-64085-351-5

Hardback: 978-1-64085-352-2

E-book: 978-1-64085-353-9

(LCCN): 2018907732

# Dedication

I dedicate this book to survivors of domestic violence, to my wonderful supportive husband and friend Scott, and to our nine children—especially my first five who survived the abuse with me. Healing happens with, through, and over time.

# Table of Contents

*Section 6: Survive: You are the prey, he is the hunter, and you don't know where he is amongst the foliage and density of his mind*

*Section 7: Revive: Restore, regain, start new towards a life of consciousness*

# Introduction

Mental illness. Addiction. Pain. Fear. Control. Abuse. What images do those words stir in your mind's eye? For me those words paint a darkening abyss filled with millions of gallons of heaviness, guilt, and duty trapping me in tangible darkness. My former spouse could not see us or find us because he was locked away in his own mind of mental illness and then became trapped by substance abuse.

He had suffered painful experiences in his childhood, and that pain warped and twisted his mind and genetic mental illness runs in his family. I share the stories as he told them to me: sometimes during drunken depressed states and other times with sober clarity, to give background. I describe abuse in two ways: the hunter and the caged animal. Both ultimately have control as the foundation. His mental illness was awakened from his pain, and as stress was added to it, he needed to control everything. How? As a caged animal strikes out at anyone to free itself; others are damaged in that process.

In nine years of marriage, we went through various stages; incredible rays of sun, to dimming light, to growing darkness, to finally inky blackness of the abyss of abuse. Why do I share this story? I write it for the victim. Why? Because there is more than hope, there is light, and I want you to know that you have worth within you more than you can ever know.

I am an author, speaker, and life strengthening coach who help the *battered, beaten, and broken* discover their *strength* to heal so that they become a victor in light! My story is what I learned as I descended into this dark abyss and how I found pinpoints of light that led me back out of it. The events that occurred will be told in the most accurate way I can: from my journals.

It brings me hope to know this book will give each reader an opportunity to learn the processes I used when escaping my abyss of abuse. My clients, their advocates, and the supporters deepen their value and their self-worth because they learn that they are WORTH it!

# SECTION 1

# Childhood Pain: When Pain is not relieved, the Results are Reckless

# CHAPTER 1

## Dusk or Dawn: Overcoming Darkness and finding Light!

Dusk or dawn? In a photograph, how can you tell if the deep pink hues of light are rising by degrees as dawn, or falling by degrees as dusk? Light in the dawn of the morning rises gently by degree minute by minute until the sun has risen filling the day with light, with warmth, and with life. Darkness, however, dims the light. As light begins to fade degree by degree the darkness begins to enfold and snuffs out the rest of the light as in dusk.

Light beckons for it to be followed. Throughout the day, you see the brightness of light; you feel warmth, energy, and heat. Darkness is black, and cold and can race from the corners of the room to snuff light out. Darkness is even tangible. Light, however, can fill a room giving it hope, heat, and brilliance. Light slices through darkness leaving a path to follow.

Light, no matter how dim, how small, can be seen through the darkness as a point to fix upon. Even in the inky tangible darkness, we can fix our eyes towards that pinpoint of light. When we use light, we can find direction through the black storms of our lives, just as lights in the harbors give safe travel around the barriers of the sea.

No one in this life is free from having dark times or trials in their lives. All darkness (no matter what caused it) feels the same for all of us. It means no light, no direction, and being hopeless.

The darkness that I faced did *not* descend all at once or like when a switch is turned off and darkness snuffs out the light suddenly. My darkness was teasing. It would feel like a dawn, but in reality, it was dusk. My dark sharp voice began in a subtle way to darken my life. The evidence that my voice of darkness was turning on me by varying degrees was so subtle it was like twilight slowly snuffing out the rays of light replacing them with degrees of darkness allowing for the black to slowly creep in. The slowness of each word and negative thought that my voice produced was another degree snuffing out the power of light and getting darker and darker was what I faced, and I suddenly realize I was in the dark.

For years the darkening power cast out my light by its powerful negative talk. I had been through counselors, through therapy, done confessions; but nothing would really penetrate that dark entanglement of thorny, sharp, thick, forest of words that barraged my brain. The entanglement was so dense that I had lost all hope of finding light or peace. If I was given a slightest flicker or flame of hope, it's cold steely breath of a word would blow it out causing gray black smoke to rise instead.

I had fallen for the trap of the negativity by believing the dark words. It was a very passive aggressive voice that I had been trying to please. I had become my inner child, weak and vulnerable. I was facing a dark demon and all I did was try to please it. I never fought the hard entanglement of words. I let the words ensnare me and pull me in to more crushing darkness. Suddenly as the last layer of darkness grabbed at me and I was ready to be snuffed out, I saw a pinpoint of light through the sharp black entanglement of thorns.

The light was like a still small voice, and it pierced me to the center of my soul. The light sliced through the sharp thorny darkness leaving a narrow pathway for me to follow. The heat of the peaceful light had seared the thorny words. The light, in this new dawn of the quiet strength from the morning, rose gently by degree minute by minute until the sun had risen filling my life with light. The sharp thorns that cut, snagged, and held me down had been severed by the light and had released me.

I started to gain focus with this ray of hope. The ray of hope had shed a new light on the things that I was currently doing: I was in college; I was exposed to new friendships and experiences with people who loved life. They had a love for things that I used to and it rekindled the fire for those things I thought I had lost in the darkness. I saw and longed for true friends who were talking with me again, I was cheering and tumbling again, and I was finding the gospel again. Those were pieces of this ray of hope; my new light.

One night I had—a dream—an awakening—I found myself floating in the air looking around me at the many choices of my life. I didn't see darkness, rather a lack of light. As the light touched my skin and radiated off my face, it felt like the sunlight of a happy memory. There was gentleness here in the white, bright light—there was also warmth. It was filling my soul.

With each step, I felt like I was home. The light held me; it encased me, it filled me, and suddenly, I felt my Heavenly

Father's loving arms around me. I was quiet in His beam of light. He allowed me, a fallen, pain filled, hurt little girl to be with Him—my Father. I was encased in this light—His light! I then began to feel a sense of my home; like my mom and dad were here supporting me and walking with me in His light. I saw others, felt others who loved me. I begin to hear the gentle strains of music that added to the light as it beckoned me forward.

Suddenly, I glanced behind me. What I saw was a tunnel of darkness, a black inky hole—void of any light—I had just come from there. I had been rescued out of the inky hole by the light. I turned my head sharply from looking behind me and focused myself on the beam of light. I enjoyed the warmth, music, and the love I was encased in. What had changed? Why had the light come? What had happened? One thing, and only one thing: there is opposition in all things; my darkness changed to light!

In my childhood and youth, I had experienced the darkness, and it was time to make a choice. I chose light. I made a choice to stop listening to the sharp dark voice that pulled me in to an entanglement of darkness. I just stopped listening—and suddenly light—Heavenly Father's appeared! I was not going to allow the dark power of my negative thoughts take me to such blackness again. I could only give my all to the light and trust in it to see where it will take me. I must trust in the light, that my Heavenly Father knows me and that His love is real, true, and that I could trust it. As I stood in that light at age 20, I saw my pinpoint ray of light; my dawn out of the darkest nights I had experienced. I left the darkness for the light!

# CHAPTER 2

# Be seen and not heard: Where is the Love?

I had been married for about seven months when I was going through some of my husband's things. My hands stroked the binding of an old photo album. As I opened it a small photo fell to the floor. It was slightly faded with age. I saw heavy dented, slightly rusty equipment and excavators rested their heavy loads on the red clay, muddy ground. In the background, scaffolding surrounded the cool gray cinder block walls. The walls teamed with tight curly black-haired workers with brown sweat-stained skin. Their skin was covered by tank-top shirts and tattered shorts. Their bare feet scrambled, clung, and stuck to everything they were climbing on. They held trowels heavy with mortar and smeared and stacked more cinder blocks adding to the wall.

The warm pacific wind gently blew off the blue waters filling the island with cooling breeze. That breeze tousled the blond hair of a four-year-old boy as the palm trees swayed in the background. The sun had burned and kissed the freckled face nose causing it to peel again and again. His eyes looked in the direction of the camera but not directly at it—just slightly beyond it.

This was one of the earliest photos I had ever seen of Thad. He was about four years old. His blond hair and freckles really stood out among the islanders. Thad spent his early years on construction sites in Fiji. The picture perfectly captured Thad's childhood: construction, being at job sites with his father, and him just looking beyond the reality that faced him.

From the stories I had heard, Thad was always seen (especially on the islands), but rarely was ever heard by his father. His father knew best. Thad's father moved the family to Fiji when Thad was a small boy. His father was in charge of several construction projects on the island and as a small child, Thad was taken to various building sites throughout the islands.

I was told that Thad's eyes would light up when he looked at the plumbing and played on the different structures like a jungle gym. He even began handing the workers their tools; his friendship with the workers was real, but soon it was time to leave and go to another site. He was to go, be seen, but not heard.

When you are not heard as a child, it leaves an imprint on you that you are not of value or of worth. As a child you feel that no one is listening, then you will figure out behaviors to make sure that you are heard. You will 1) act out, 2) yell, 3) repeat yourself, 4) talk softly forcing people to listen, or 5) stop talking all together and retreat in to your mind to avoid the pain of rejection. Do any of these feel familiar? Pain will motivate people to do what they can to numb it,

> *When you are not heard as a child, it leaves an imprint on you that you are not of value or of worth.*

run from it, or deal with it. The pain that was deep in my former husband began in his childhood years. I only heard a few of those pain-filled stories when we were married. He shared this story with me during a particular night of pain.

Sitting on the woven mat cross-legged, five-year-old Thad tried to hold still. "Sit!" was the final word of the teacher. She was a large woman, hair pinned up with a large teak wooden comb and wearing her regular floral Muumuu. Thad's wiggles and movements came from deep down inside and seemed to control him. As he tried to sit cross-legged, he grabbed the sides of his pant legs with his small calloused hands trying and willing himself to hold still. His freckled face and blue eyes stood out of the dark sea of black hair and chocolate eyes. He was the outsider, the one that didn't seem to fit; the trouble-maker. He shut his eyes and held the sides of his pants tighter. He would not move! He did not want to be "tabled", again.

The teacher was reading a story to the class. All the children sat with him on the woven mat as an ocean breeze gently blew across the room through the open windows. Her booming voice was loud and was laced with mockery as she read the story. She knew the words, and the children didn't. She knew the letters, and the children didn't. She knew the counting, and the children didn't. For her, the control of the classroom was her power; not the knowledge she should have been imparting.

Suddenly, through the open window a small island bird flew in landing on a shelf. The bird nodded and looked side to side and up and down until it seemed to catch Thad's eye. Thad's eyes followed the moment of the bird as the teacher's booming voice began to move from the forefront to the background of his mind.

The story seemed to fade away and the colorful feathers of that bird seemed to get brighter and as Thad's eyes stared, the colors seemed to invite him to take a closer look. He leaned forward and looked with intent. The striking blue head, red crested chest, light splash of green on the back the neck, and the darker green wings of the bird seemed to call at him—drawing him in bit by bit. He watched the bird's head bob up and down and the teacher's voice faded and faded. He could see the colors up close and the textures of the smooth feathers as they blended together green. He reached out to touch and suddenly the bird took flight! It was as if the spell had been broken and he was back in the classroom.

Thad found himself *off* the woven mat and on the other side of the classroom next to the bookshelf. There was no booming voice—it had faded to silence. There was no story in the background, and the dark faces of his classmates were staring at him, not beside him. He could not believe how he had gotten there by the shelf. He quickly shut his eye and said to himself, *He was on the mat!* He was on the mat! He willed it to be true. He was on the mat—not next to the shelf. The mat!

Suddenly Thad's feet were lifted off the floor and he found himself standing on the table! The voice boomed loud for all the class. The shaming of the blonde freckled face outcast had begun—again. He was not to be followed, he was not a leader, and he was trouble! Since this was Thad's third offense, he was told to pull down his pants and stand in his underwear while the class laughed and the teacher boomed more shaming words to which no one came to rescue him from.

Why no rescue? The way that Thad shared it with me he said that no one listened. He explained that once while headed towards a construction site, Thad told his dad what school was like and what being "*tabled*" meant. His dad turned to him and said, "then pay attention and you won't be *tabled*." That was it. The gavel had been struck. Thad's story—his words—did nothing: no sympathy, no support, no talking to the teacher, and no emotional rescue for Thad. Thad was to be seen and not heard.

## CHAPTER 3

# The Fort: How Dreams Shatter

One dark night in October 2001, Thad shared this next story with me during one of his sober pain filled nights. We had been married for 4 years when he shared this story with me. Through his hate filled and shame filled words he shared this story with me.

Upon returning from the Islands, his father moved the family to a little piece of country. They lived on a large one-acre plot of land with a backyard that spilled down a large hill and into a gully filled with grasses, scrub oak, and animals. This was Thad's version of heaven. He had space to run, things to do, and time to create!

Being essentially alone, Thad needed things to do and places to explore. Socially, Thad had a few friends in elementary school, a few at church, but as time went on, his friendships dwindled due to his social awkwardness, so he sought refuge in his mind and with what he could create.

The creative process came quickly for Thad as the family began construction on their new home. His life was consumed by construction as his dad built the house brick by brick. During that time, Thad was almost always found outside, exploring, building, tinkering, inventing, and creating something. He was always making things with his hands and he was successful at it. He was very bright and knew how things worked. He also tinkered with things until he figured it out.

He said that at seven years old, Thad decided to build a fort in the gully. Thad scavenged his home job site for things he could use: discarded boards, nails, tools etc. Some days he just couldn't find what he needed. Many of his scavenger days, he'd biked down the hill on towards the gas station for candy, soda, or for things he would need for his projects. Each time he would pass a dumpy old garage packed full of treasures! He would slow down just to get a peek at the boards, the old glass windows, the old doors, and so forth.

One spring Saturday morning when Thad went down the hill, he noticed someone in the garage. He applied his brakes on his bike and slowed down long enough to see his neighbor. The man looked up and smiled at Thad. Thad waved and smiled as he went past. Thad went passed the old garage a few more Saturdays until finally one day, he stopped at the open door of the garage and walked in.

Thad's seven-year-old eyes had fallen upon a treasure trove of building possibilities: boards, rusty tools, nails, wavy glass, a wagon wheel, rusted plow, and six panel doors with the door knob that still worked! The neighbor suddenly appeared from behind an old chest of drawers. He was wiping off white slime from his calloused hands on a mangy rag, brushed the sweat off his grimy brow, and with a zipper sound, adjusted himself then stepped out to meet Thad. That was the first time the two met, and it would not be their last.

Thad was a trusting kid; he was essentially friendless, and he always needed things for his projects. Soon a relationship was formed, and trust was built between him and the neighbor. When Thad's dad was too busy with the family house, Thad would ask for advice on his project from his neighbor. Spring melted in to early summer, his trips to the garage were more and more frequent. Thad's tinkering around in the garage to find more tools and ideas for his projects meant that time he spent with the neighbor increased as well and weeks gave in to months.

The slow heat of July gave way in to the depths of an August summer. With his bare feet, a dry, brown, hot, dusty, trail was kicked up by a seven-year-old. The blond sweep of hair was being tossed back by a cool breeze rising up out of the gully. The freckled face hung down with blue eyes fixed on the dirt trail as he stepped closer to home. With his eyes cast downward, he saw the white salty blotchy stain was still on his pant leg. He froze where he stood and looked at that stain.

He quickly reached down and grabbed a handful of dead grass and tried to brush it off. It was just smearing it on to his hands and deeper in to his pant leg. Looking at his hands he could see the stain was also in between his fingers. His stomach dropped. Why had he gone back to the garage? He needed just a few more nails to finish the fort. The quick trip to garage for those nails to finish his fort was just supposed to be like all the others over the summer: say hi, grab a few nails, and out the door to finish the project. However, this trip in to the dark garage was like none other.

The garage was a place of trust. It was a place to find the materials, gain advice on how to nail the boards, how to fix the windowpane, and the doorknob. That garage had helped him to form The Fort—The Fort had been the project for the summer. Since his father was too busy to help because of all the work on their personal house, Thad sought the advice of his neighbor. With his own hands he had drawn his very first of many house plans, but now these hands were stained with dirt and slippery goo.

He continued to kick up the dirt as he walked the long walk home, while he continued to rub his hands clean of the experience in the garage. He simply trudged through the gully up the sunbaked hill, to his home never to return to The Fort again.

The neighbor, the garage, the acts that happened there was never talked about. He never told anyone. He kept the secret for nearly two decades.

When Thad told me about the abuse, he had a sense of shame in his voice as he told me the story. I remember looking in his eyes. They were wrinkled with pain. I saw the tender feelings of him wanting to feel loved, but instead the emotions of pain and shame was all that he could feel.

The demands from the neighbor and the emotional damage it caused Thad rolled in to him like a dark, deep, cold, ocean wave pounding against the side of a ship ready to take it down to the bottom of the sea. That emotional damage and the pain that it caused had to be dealt with in either healthy or unhealthy ways, and unfortunately the unhealthy way was chosen.

## CHAPTER 4

# Light and Darkness: Why Pain pushes us to Numb Out

Light and Darkness: they are the extreme opposites of each other. After my husband shared his story of abuse, I began to understand why he escaped, why he ran, why he felt powerless, and why he pushed to be numbed out. The darkness and pain of sexual abuse is so damaging that our minds and hearts spend a lifetime trying to process the feelings and hopefully find healing. It takes work to leave the darkness and the pain of life and go towards the light. For Thad, the darkness of his pain led him towards another path. It was complex for Thad. He was lost, hurt, and in pain from the neighbor, from failures in school, and from not being accepted for who he was.

He chose to numb his pain with drugs and alcohol. He once described it to me as darkness—like when a switch is turned off and darkness snuffs out the light completely. He said it was like being a miner in a cave or a mine watching the final flicker of light from the stub of candle dance, wave, and be snuffed out. The darkness was deep and cold. He felt like he was stumbling around feeling his way along the jagged walls of the cave. He felt a deep black shadow slowly creeping behind him. The shadow snuffed out the small flicker of light he had within himself until he suddenly realized his soul was captured the inky tangible darkness of something—something heavy! It was addiction.

How did his addiction start? In high school, and it was described like this:

Ready? His friends called out. He put his lips around the joint and took in a deep, deeper, fight the pain of the heat as it seared his throat, draw on the joint. He kept drawing in the smoke until the last space in his lungs filled; hold it! And let it out.... with each deflating of the lung filled with the artificial exhilaration now raced and ripped through his brain like a dull bullet numbing him to the reality about him.

Numb. He tuned in the noises he heard: it was drunken laughter and silly music. His dull mind kept tuning in to the sound, and joined in. He was numb! He had arrived at his pleasure place thanks to the power of the vapors and magic of smoke. "Stay! Live here", employed the drug. It was a powerfully intense feeling. Thad said it was like a stretchy, flexible wall--like everything is made of plastic. He would push on that wall—did you see it give in; even bounce? The power of the smoke gives this all to you! Enjoy—escape life!

During his intense moments of being high he would feel the lust and desire to have sex. He described sex when he was high as if he was pressing on the bouncy wall again and would reached around it. He would call out to his girlfriend to come and "play." She was against the springy wall and flashed a smile at him. He would look at her, the glitter and the shine from her face, and he would place his hand on the springy wall and give in to it. He touched her and he looked long and hard in to the eyes that blinked and flirted with him. He reached for her, took her, pulled her in; she was smiling at him. Then suddenly she would give him a kiss, a hot wet kiss. From the trigger of that kiss, his hands felt her curves and smooth skin.

The touch of that skin made him hunger for more and soon, his skin was against hers. His kiss went deeper and suddenly he was connected. He heard only her desire; the power of the vapors/drugs and her power had him hooked.

Then as he felt the intense lust of the sex connection between him and the girl, he suddenly felt cold steel-like fingers squeezing tightness of a cable all about him. His connection was broken from the girl, and her shrill laughter cut him in mocking waves as the cold cable made from the smoke and vapors grasped him. It tightened, ripping in to him as he struggled to pull away. He tried to pull back and find a way to fill his lungs with fresh air and some light.

As he gasped for a breath, he sucked in the putrid acid taste of vomit and of ashes from an ashtray. He sputtered, gasped, and fought to be free of the drug cable that seems to be cutting at his flesh. He turned his head sharply to get away from the smell of sick and smoke. The sound of laughter from his drug high turned to screaming and shrieking! The dreamy music from the richness of the vapor had turned to intense horror! The lights from the drug party had gone black and he symbolically felt wet hardness underneath him. The drugs and the sexual encounters have turned on him and thrown him out. He was in the dark, the cold, and with no one. Alone.

Being sexually curious as a youth and experimenting with drugs seems like a rite of passage for many people growing up. It's just something to do and then you leave that behind you and move on to adulthood. But for Thad who was pushing down and trying to numb out pain, it suddenly trapped him! He described it that it felt like steel cables that were around his body as the high of the drug left him and the crash of despair enveloped him. He fought for breath, for air, for a way out, but the darkening pressure held him to what felt like wet concrete as if pulled there by a magnet.

The blackness, the pressure that was crushing his lungs the icy coldness; suddenly he screamed out with the last breath he had, and he was frozen in a cold dark place. He was in the drug's power. He was also trapped in sin. He strained his eyes frantically about to see anything in the inky-blackness— NOTHING! Then suddenly, he turned his eyes upward as he felt his body being pulled downward and he saw a pinpoint of light. Thad was given some hope for the first time! He had a friend. A real friend helped him to feel the love of Jesus in his life.

He said that once he made up his mind to repent and turn towards the Savior, it felt like the following:

He stretched his mind towards that infinitesimal pin-prick of light hoping to be saved from the crushing cold inky blackness he was in. The light was there above him! He was stretching and reaching out to it again! The light was getting brighter, steadier. More pinpricks of light seem to penetrate the darkness like a galaxy of stars slowly filling the night sky. The light dispels the grasp of darkness pushing and straining the blackness back to the corners of the room.

He described it as more and more pinpoints of light he could see; they would strengthen in to a beam of light. The narrow beam of light connected with more beams, and the beams had melted in to rays and the rays filled and filled the black space he was in until he realized he could feel the heat of the light through his skin as it began to fill a room giving it hope and brilliance.

Thad was in the pit of the deepest darkest drug of despair and then he was surrounded by light! Who casts this light? Who was filling this room with warmth, with light, with peace? He said he saw the faces of those he loved: his mother, his siblings, even his father, and a few friends.

Then the feeling of peace began to wash over him like a warm bath. He felt cleansed, pure, clean again, and as he turned towards his source of light, he saw a face, a face of love, a face that wanted him to stay in His light, His glory, and His love. His light shines forth and he basked in this light and He asked Thad to follow Him. Thad said he felt lost; an addict filled with sin. But, The Lord shone His light towards him again and he knew the answer: repent and live.

Over time and line upon line, Thad worked through the pain and the shame because of His light. He confessed his sins because he wanted to stay in that light! The work, the pain, the praying, the confessions, the changing of his behavior—it was all worth it!

The light of forgiveness now fully shone on him, and he was clean. He explained it to me that as he turned towards Jesus, he knew he needed to serve Him. Thad vowed to stay here in the light and to never return to the darkness; to never fall back into the powerful hands of drugs, alcohol, or sex outside of marriage again.

Thad's journey back towards and finding the saving grace of the Lord Jesus Christ was a hard long road. As he left those addictions through the power of prayer, confession, the priesthood, and the power of forgiveness from Jesus Christ's Atonement, he felt whole. He felt healed. Some of his physical and some emotional scars from the past were still seen by others, but only he felt the depth of that pain. Unfortunately, he was judged and marked by his past by many. Some people were not trusting that he would really ever leave addiction behind—that he had truly repented and found a new path.

What draws us towards others is shared common experiences and then gaining understanding, sympathy, and empathy from others based on those experiences. Many people, who have experienced that world of addiction, are the only ones that can truly understand the pain of recovery. If you have been in the world of addiction, abuse, or adultery, it is a tough past to leave. No one can know the pain and the damage that those scars carried for Thad other than Thad himself. But we can learn to love others who have changed their ways and have left their past behind them.

> *What draws us towards others is shared common experiences and then gaining understanding, sympathy, and empathy from others based on those experiences.*

Thad and I had a common scar between us. We had both been fallen angels—molested as children. (My journey and story will not be shared here, but in a different book: Light, Love & Lack). The abuse was done by a neighbor, someone who had built trust with us and then shattered it for their own selfish gain. From that abuse, we both had different ways to cope with the pain of it. The scarring that happened to us is deep on many levels. The abuse of a child that happens through touch, through pictures, through actions, through games, through threats, and through words will leave pain and a lifetime of healing. The very acts of the abuse are stimulating and shaming at the same time, and it takes time to understand that we are not broken, discarded, or trash.

The tug and pull between God's given gift of procreation and the abuse/control of another are extreme opposites of each other therefore causing the victim to harbor intense damage. The degree of abuse is damaging to the victim, and victims spend a lifetime swimming through the emotional tidal waves of shame and guilt trying to find ways to understand it, and to try to heal from it.

The darkness of Thad's shame and pain led him to drugs, alcohol, and a porn addiction. My pain and shame led me to control food and trying to please others. Why was there all this pain? Was it from the pain of the molestation? Was it from the pain of never fitting in? Was it from the pain of not having friends? Possibly all of that, but I'll never know the depth of it. What I do know is that Thad and I both used destructive methods to cope with the pain and anxiety of our individual realities. As Thad's light was turned down by degrees because of his choices, he found himself in the darkening pit with little to no choices.

But just as darkness had engulfed him, he was saved by light. The light that was cast on him came from so many on his behalf: his mother, his family, his Bishop, and his Savior. He clung to that feeling of being cleansed. He knew the opposition in all things; he had known the difference. He had made covenants to remain in the light and to serve his Heavenly Father on his mission.

What did I learn about Thad when I learned what he had gone through to be clean to serve his mission? I learned that he could get through hard things if he focused and used the Lord for help. That was something that attracted me to him.

# SECTION 2:

# The Attraction: Similarities, commonalities, and convenience draw people together

CHAPTER 5

# Mission Garden: You reap what you Sow

I've learned that things happen for a reason, that the "every-day events" all have value and meaning. Those events give us times to laugh or strength to improve ourselves when we are in trials. I will admit that sometimes when I am in the middle of a trial, I don't always remember that or I can't really see how the hard times are going to help me, but overall, with hindsight, it usually does.

Thad and I met in Southern California. He was serving as a missionary for the Church of Jesus Christ of Latter-Day Saints and so was I. During our missionary service in Southern California, we were in a similar geographic area for about one month. We would see each other at missionary meetings, but we worked in different areas of the city.

In the area where Thad served there was space to build a little garden. His companion was the zone leader, meaning, he was in charge of the missionaries in that area and he spent time on the phone taking the reports from the other missionaries. The mission rules are that companions are to stay together at all times. Since his companion was busy with reports and Thad needed to keep himself busy, he got permission to plant a garden.

The little garden; it had just been a small project something to keep Thad busy while his companion attended to the needs of the zone leadership. He kept an eye on it daily: tilling, weeding, and weekly watering the garden. It was so simple, but so profound for me as my mission in that geographic area wore on.

Early in the spring Thad scraped, shoveled, stepped, pulled back, lifted, and turned the dirt over, again and again. Shovels of brown and red clay dirt mix were laid as his hands gripped the shovel that tilled the little patch of earth. Soon from those little seeds sprouted little tuffs of green in neat little rows throughout the garden. The little tufts grew up in to the different plants and vines: cucumbers, peppers, squash, tomatoes, peas, and beans. It was all planted entirely by him and harvested throughout the summer by many of us missionaries. We loved the garden and the fresh food it provided for so many of us.

I personally became in need of this garden in the summer of 1996. I had become ill on my mission. My illness? My body's digestive system was not doing what it should. It was slowing down to a crawl and my body was filling up with toxins. I could not expel the toxins because my digestion was so slow and I was miserable. I could finally take the pain from the bloating and cramping any longer and sought for medical help.

Emotionally and physically seeking out medical help for my discomfort was a painful process for me. It was very embarrassing to learn that my illness was caused by my fight with food—the anorexia. My actions had damaged my digestion, and now on my mission, the consequence of this damage was being played out. I had gained 15 pounds in one month all due to water and waste that was not being properly expelled from my system. I was filling up with toxins and I was sick! I had three scopes performed to see the intense damage that was caused, and to see what I could do to get better.

As I sat in the office following the procedure and the doctor had asked his barrage of questions about what I ate, what I didn't eat, what I was allergic to; all I could think about was how stupid I had been. I gave him the answers to the questions he was asking and my mind and heart were numb because all the answers had pulled me back to the days of my food fights and my anorexia battle. Those were dark and emotional scars that I had to live through again as I answered the embarrassing questions of how I controlled food to control my pain.

Following the questioning, the answer was that I had done damage to my body by my "coping mechanism", and now the consequences of my actions were being played out in my gut. What was the answer—the physical cure? I needed to heal my gut by giving it stimulation. Here were my options: 1) surgery to remove the damaged portions, which also meant I would have to leave my missionary service, or 2) I could try intensive stimulation therapy, stool softeners, fiber, and try to fix my digestion through nutrition. If I choose the second option I would have two months to see if I was able to see if the therapy would work. If it did not, then my missionary service would be finished.

I sat in stunned silence in that office. It was as if the world had closed off from me and started to dim. I quickly found myself in a place of prayer pleading with Heavenly Father to stay on my mission so that I could serve him. I wanted to stay. The second option was the only option. I wanted to stay to serve my Heavenly Father. I knew I could be healed, and that I could bring others to Him through His word and through His Atonement.

I sat in more silence. I wanted to stay on my mission. I knew I could get the help I needed through prayer, exercise, and the new strict diet. I knew I could only do that by eating fresh fruits and veggies, and grains. More silence. I knew that my body could be healed. I knew that my mistakes could be reversed if I followed the diet. I knew that I could stay and serve my Heavenly Father through my missionary service if I followed what was being told to me. This would be hard work. There was no magic in it, but I was determined to stay. I needed real food water, fiber, and exercise to help stimulate the bowel. I hoped this would get me back on track. This was something that I could do. I told the doctor I was going to do option two.

The silence that surrounded me left and I found myself walking away from that office with real lessons learned and an opportunity to find more healing and strength with this program. I felt great relief and hope, but now I needed to find a way to afford the fresh veggies.

When I understood the answers to my illness, that was when I learned of the little garden that Thad had started. The Mission Garden was there for all of us, and now personally for me. Thad felt that he was growing it not just as a project but for something more, and now he knew why. I thanked him and told him how grateful I was for his little garden. It was one mile away, and my companion and I would go and harvest the garden, as we needed. I ate the veggies harvested from the garden through the summer and it helped my gut to flourish again. It was simple. It was there, and I felt Thad had been inspired to plant it for a good cause, and that good cause happened to be me. It was a little love grown in a garden for me in Southern California.

What did I learn? I learned that there was a cause and effect to all my actions whether emotional or physical. I had caused damage to my body when I sought to control my pain, but when I gave my pain over to the Lord, my life was better.

CHAPTER 6

# Love Grows: Love Can Change You for a Time

"Goodbye." Click. A quick giggle welled up inside me. I released my hand from off the receiver and placed the phone back in to its cradle. I thought to myself, *I didn't even think that anyone knew I was back from my mission.* I had only been back in Utah for 48 hours. That was fast! How did he know I was back? I guess missionaries like to stick together. I was still surprised, and another set of giggles escaped. *I guess I'll see them all on Sunday at my homecoming,* I thought.

When I returned home from my mission in December of 1996, Thad was one of the first people who called me. He called me and asked if he could come to my Homecoming and bring some fellow returned missionaries with him. I thought that this would be great to see everyone again and didn't think much beyond that. Following my Homecoming meeting, we had a get-together afterward and we were able to talk and mingle. Thad and the other friends stayed and talked. We all had a great time.

After that day, Thad basically never left. He would call, and we would talk and talk on the phone. We would share and remember experiences from the mission. Those were good calls; nice times. We got to know each other through the conversations and it was great to have someone who shared similar experiences.

As the winter wore on, Thad and I called each other nearly every night to talk about our day, our feelings, and the awful blind dates that we had been set upon. It was so nice to have someone that understood how strange it was to change from missionary work yet trying to get in to the everyday workings of life again. There was a lot in common for us as we would talk about those experiences and soon more than a friendship developed. We started to kind of grow on each other.

"Thanks for going with me. It was really good to see you again," said Thad as he held my hand and walked me back to my house. My hand felt two small hand pumps as his strong hand held onto mine and he cradled my back with his other hand. We walked up to my door. I turned to him and gave him a smile.

"It was nice to see you. I had a great time. It was nice to laugh. It was great to see the wedding reception of our missionary friends. Thanks again", I said. It had been a great night filled with laughter and reminiscing about the mission, sharing stories of faith, of the people we both loved dearly, and about the area we had known over the past two years. There was a lot in common there and he and I shared in that joyfully together.

We both smiled at each other again, and then he reached in and gave me a kiss on the cheek. I turned to him and smiled again. "Call you tomorrow?" he asked, "Sure," came my reply. And with a final hand squeeze and then a release, I watched him walk back to the car. I slowly turned the knob, stepped in to my house, and gently closed the door leaning my back against the door. Sigh...it was a wonderful night.

That night led to other nights and in the whirlwind courtship and conversations, came one conversation that I'll never forget. Thad and I went on a drive through a beautiful mountain valley. In that valley, Thad said that he wanted to talk to me about his past and without mincing any words, he bluntly began. He told me that he did not finish high school. He told me that he had done drugs and alcohol in high school. He even told me about his girlfriend and about all the sex. He was very truthful and blunt. As the miles wore on in the beautiful valley, I knew that I had to decide. I thanked him for being blunt and honest with me. I told him I would be quiet for a few days to really think about things and figure out what all of this would mean to me.

He dropped me off after that long ride, and I did just that. I went quiet for a few days. I was waiting to hear what my heart was going to tell me. I prayed to know if this was still right to keep going out with Thad. My answer was always, "he was truthful with you. He wanted you to know up front. He wanted me to know." I remember taking time to think about it. I remember praying and trying to figure out if his past was his past and if Thad had moved on, had repented, and had been forgiven.

After a few days' time, I felt that Thad's past was in the past. That Thad had changed and that the Thad I knew, at the time, was nothing like that. He was committed to the gospel, a hard worker, and he was willing to give up anything for our relationship. I believe that people can repent, change, and improve their circumstances through the Atonement of Jesus Christ, and I felt that Thad had done that.

Thad explained how he had worked through the drugs and alcohol problems and made all of this right before he went to serve his mission. I felt that he was telling me the truth. For me, if you have changed your ways with sincere repentance, then you have changed your ways. The sin is forgiven, and it is time to press forward. That phrase "press forward" was all that Thad would talk about. He did not want to repeat the past. He, with tears and with sincerity, would plead with me to live the way the Lord wanted us. A few weeks following that conversation Thad asked me to marry him. I accepted. We were engaged.

During our courtship, Thad was adamant that we attend the Temple weekly. He would say that even though he had been through so much, that "as long as we focused ourselves on the temple, we would not fall in to Satan's grasp." Again, I believed that. I trusted things when it came to forgiveness with the Lord. I trusted those conversations. I felt that it was true.

The engagement and courtship were fast. We needed an apartment to live in, and Thad's dad offered us a way to find an apartment. He offered that if we did the work, that we could finish the basement of their home, and live there rent-free. All during our engagement, we built the apartment. The basement of his parent's home was going to be our starting point. This is where we would live, grow and love together, and be married.

Tick, tick, ticking of the clock—waiting for the pipe glue to dry; it was 11:22 pm. Twist another piece into place, make the angle and turn the elbow bend into place. Tick, tick, tick...it was now nearing midnight. Gears grinding, motor humming, and the whirring sound of the concrete mixer rang out through the night: scrape, slide, pinging off the rocks and sliding sound of the sand and concrete mixture. We added the water and the wet sound seemed to drop the mixer in to a lower gear and pitch, and the slosh of the mixture slopped round and round.

Soon the spinning slowed, and we dumped the gray heavy slop in to the wheelbarrow from the mixer. Thad strained as he grasped the handles and felt his muscles in his forearms contract as he pushed up the ramp with the heavy slop from the garage to the new bathroom. He lifted and dumped the mixture into the trench. He did two more wheelbarrow loads: lift, push, and dump. Together we watched the mix hug and smother the pipe in to its grasp and began hardening it into place. Then Thad's thick forearms and rough hands used the trowel and scraped, smoothed, troweled, scraped, and frosted the mixture smooth.

Tick, tick, tick, 1:00 am, Thad's knees buckled, and he sat on the floor. Exhaustion. I wiped my forehead smearing the gray mixture across it and flopped down next to him. We sat with our backs against the roughly framed walls, painting with exhaustion. Then turned to each other with tired heavy eyes and smiles. We had been working since about 7 am, and all the plumbing was finished in the basement. Together. We could do anything together.

With each phase of building the basement apartment, I could see that Thad had a talent for construction and a gift to create something from nothing. He was like a kid in a candy shop working with all the tools: measuring, cutting, nailing, plumbing, wiring, and the finish work. I loved watching him work. It was where I saw his most honest self, and it was a wonderful way to spend our engagement.

The weeks quickly passed during our engagement, and it was a time to grow and love each other. As Thad and I brushed the last strokes of paint on the casing we looked at each other deeply. He smiled and pulled me close and kissed my head. I rested my head on his chest, and we just stood there knowing that if we were honest and depended on each other, we would make it.

Our married life began as many do. The engagement, the building of the apartment, spending time together, and then a wedding ceremony that pulled us through to our marriage. The weeks following our Temple wedding were filled with love as we got to know each other.

One day following a challenging day of work and summer school, I came home early to just find some rest out of the heat. I slipped off my shoes, took off my necklace, and put it on the dresser when I noticed an envelope addressed "To my future wife." I turned it over and ran my finger under the dried glue and slipped open the envelope. I unfolded the three pages that had been so neatly tucked into place and sat on the bed to read.

The words that had been penned on that paper fell on my heart in loving waves of gratitude, love, and truth. My smile gently spread across my face and my heart was swollen with what I read. It was a love letter. It was a powerful letter confessing his love for me and for our future family. I read and reread that letter. I have never had such an honest expression of love given to me. I kept the letter and hid it in my treasure box for me to pull out and read when I needed reminding of the love he had for me. Several other letters were written to me during that first year of marriage and they were held close to my heart as a precious reminder that he truly loved me. I was worth loving. I was worth caring for. And, I was honored to be his wife.

*The words that had been penned on that paper fell on my heart in loving waves of gratitude, love, and truth.*

Even with all of my dark flaws in the past, from that beginning point in our marriage, I could be loved for me. That was the truth—and that was light. I could be forgiven for my shortcomings and I would do the same for him. That's what love does. We had a stable footing of faith, love, and of life ahead of us. Love could grow as we both worked on the relationship of marriage together, and for us, the love did grow—for a time.

34

## CHAPTER 7

# Gotcha! Knights Rescue their Damaged Damsels in Distress

I had been married for around three months when early one morning, I got up to shower and prepare for the day. I crawled out from under the covers and crept quietly in to the bathroom as to let Thad sleep. I looked back at him sound asleep in bed. I didn't want to wake him. I undressed and turned on the water for the shower. As I stepped up in to the tub, my footing hit the slime of soap that was in the bottom of the tub. My foot shot out from underneath me and propelled me with enough force that pushed my upper body out in to a different direction. I began to fall.

It felt like I was descending in slow motion. I could see the tile coming in to deeper focus, almost feel the ground coming closer to me. I saw the pattern of the tile the corner of the white flashing before me! I had nothing to brace myself with, and down I continued. I was getting ready for the impact, but instead, I felt calloused hands—strong and safe underneath my head. "Gotcha!" Thad caught my head before I hit it on the tile.

We were both shaking! His eyes were wild with fright and his deep breaths kept going in and out at a fast pace. I looked into those blue eyes as he looked into mine. He embraced me and repeated over and over, "I thought you were going to die!" We stayed locked together until we were calm. He was my knight rescuing his damsel in distress.

Why was this event of Thad catching me so important? It was just a slip in the shower, no big deal, but for us, it was a big deal. My grandmother had fallen and struck her head on a piece of furniture a few weeks before that and did not recover. She eventually passed away due to complications of that head injury. I think with that event so fresh in our minds, my slipping and falling felt like the same peril.

I didn't realize how in tune Thad was to the Spirit until that moment. He was in bed asleep. Then in an instant, he was catching my head before it cracked on the tile. I asked him how he knew that I was in trouble. He said he simply heard a voice tell him to go—go now! He ran and saw me falling, and that was it. I called him throughout the day and thanked him over and over again.

> I didn't realize how in tune Thad was to the Spirit until that moment.

This event was a foundation for how we treated each other. We loved each other so much that we were first in each other's thoughts. We were growing together, trusting each other, and following the direction of the Lord. This is all I ever wanted. To build a life together in honesty with trust, work, and love, and we were doing it.... for a while.

# SECTION 3

*Thrills: When you witness the creative brilliance of someone, it is a thrill!*

# CHAPTER 8

# Additions: Growing Pains, Births, and Warnings

My hands loving stroked the hand turned rungs of the bassinet. I gently tipped the curved legs watching the cherry stain wooden rocker rock back and forth. Gently his hands slipped behind me wrapping around my expanding waist. I leaned against him as my hand continued to rock. The smell of freshly cut pinewood and the lights casting a soft glow over the living room made our first Christmas together one to remember.

As we stood in that embrace, I thought about all of the blessings we had: our first child, "our addition", would be born in July. I was graduating from the University with my four-year degree. Thad and his father were building a spec home that would be completed by June, so we had a steady income. As the snow fell outside, we stayed safe and warm in the apartment that we had built and where we found our love for each other. Suddenly there was a knock at the apartment door. That knock shattered our little moment and suddenly the door opened. It was my father-in-law.

The moment Thad and I just had experienced was over. Whenever my father-in-law knocked on the door, it was to announce his entrance; it was not to ask permission. Following the knock, he would just come in whether we said to come in or not. My father-in-law had his "let's talk business" face on. I knew what that meant. Thad was going to rehash the spec home all over again: What to do, how to sell it, why it wasn't selling, what the next phase of construction was going to be, and what was going to happen if they didn't sell it. I sighed and went to the bedroom. These business talks never left Thad calm; they stressed him out.

Thad did not return to the bedroom until later that night. Christmas Day was gone like the rays of the day, not to return for another year. We had had a moment, but it was interrupted by what my father-in-law needed. I sighed and snuggled deep in to the layers of quilts of my cocoon waiting for the empty day of the 26th to arrive.

With the holidays over and the winter months in full swing, Thad's building process went from outside to inside. The progress on the spec home was coming along great. The progress with my belly, the addition, was also doing well. We just would bide our time through the long winter and make plans for his business, for the baby, and for our future.

Thad and I had great conversations together (minus all the times my father-in-law would need to "talk business") about our future life with our addition. With my school ending and his spec home coming to an end, we were faced with many different options on what to do for our family: 1) Finish the spec home and stay in the basement for another year to continue to save money and then move out on our own. 2) Finish the spec home and then move to Idaho for Thad to go to school and to be on our own. 3) Invest in some properties in Idaho to rent out as a source of income. Or 4) sell the spec home and reinvest the money with his dad for another spec home.

Many of the options were discussed and we both had a feeling that we needed to leave the basement apartment, but to do what and to go where? That was still a toss-up. Should we go to Idaho? But we don't really know anyone. It was such a change. How would Thad get work? What would I do with a newborn there? Shouldn't we stay close to the family? We were attending the temple twice a month and taking this question to the Lord there. No clear answer was coming, other than we knew we needed to leave the basement. These were the conversations that went round and round for months, and stress was building. It would flash across his face and his knuckles would whiten, and then fade.

Since we both felt the need to leave the apartment, we started thinking about the idea of moving into the spec home as our first home. With my "nesting" drive from the pregnancy, the idea caught me on fire! Thad had been actively trying to sell the home the entire time he was building it, but there were just no bites. After building it for nine months and still not having someone to buy it, we decided to take over the loan and move in. We thought that it would be an investment in the business. We would keep it for sale and sell it as soon as we could.

The idea of the home became something I could not let go of. I don't always give myself time to think about decisions because the overall drive can override it. I have a great imagination, energy, and enthusiasm and this idea of having a home became an obsession for me. I wanted to have a place for our little family and for us to keep going and growing together without the constant interruption of my father-in-law.

So, I pushed Thad to see if we could get out of the basement and move. He was nervous and hesitant, but I thought for sure that it would be a goal to work towards that would help keep us focused on what we needed to do. I just felt that it was going to work out. There were only two times I saw the knuckles whiten with his clenched fists, but it always left—it was a warning, but I focused elsewhere. We moved into the home on July third, and three days later our son, Kellis, was born. Our child, our addition had come home.

Time has a way of being consistent and yet passing. Time ticks by every second, minute, hour, day, week, month, and year. Days turn in to nights and the pattern repeats to build weeks and months. Being a new mommy and Thad being the breadwinner, our lives became a different kind of busy. The drive Thad had to get whatever type of construction job he could was the full focus for our survival. I did my best to make the home a place of comfort and love for the new men in my lives: Thad and my son. Life has a way of ticking by and changing habits simply because we run out of time.

Our weekly time at the temple had passed to two times a month at the temple. Two times a month at the temple had dropped down to once a month. The saying is true, "the sun will come out tomorrow", but for us, our days of working together, and temple worship together were slowly starting to turn. Life with a child, a mortgage, a personal business, church callings, and family, brought about stress. Our together time and the time we spent in the temple was less and less.

Stress is an interesting fact of life. It happens to us all, yet we all handle it differently. I know that Satan knows our weakness and he seems to be able to tempt us in the most stressful places of our lives. Instead of running to a place of peace like the temple, Thad and I were consumed with how to survive and our temple time together dropped to three times a year. Thad and I had built our courtship, our engagement, and our first year of marriage around the ability to attend the temple once a week. During our engagement, he said, "as long as we focus ourselves on the temple, we will not fall in to Satan's grasp."

Additions—we had a lot of them: more bills, business financial stress, work, job finding, and deadlines. Deadlines: soon we found out that another special deadline in late October would come. Since we had taken on the mortgage just to get out under my father-in-law's foot, the worry was now of getting the next build job to feed not just three of us but soon four of us. The news of another addition did not bring joy; it brought a shadow and a warning. The stress just kept on mounting and building no matter what I tried to do. I felt I was in an unfamiliar place and did not know how to act in this gray zone of his silence. This was only the beginning of our journey towards the darkness of our marriage. It was the beginning in a subtle way; however, the darkness would soon enfold us until it held us captured in its grasp.

# CHAPTER 9

## The Party: A Shadow Awakens

The pressure of a business, a wife, a mortgage, and one and a half children is a lot to take on at 24 years old, but there we were. My hands plunged into the hot soapy water searching for the bottle to wash. My eyes were focused out the west-facing window through the slits in the blinds and on to the walnut tree of the neighbor's yard. My hands mechanically pumped the sponge up and down the neck of the bottle when I heard the squeak of the tires. I took in a deep breath to steady myself. Those were the brakes of my father-in-law. He was here to talk to Thad again. Again. Again. Nothing new came from these chats, just a time to rehash the problems and have no solutions—a loop like a record that is finished playing and you only hear the static popping sound repeating again and again in an irritating fashion.

That loop had no goal. No outcome. Without the goal, the work, and effort, anyone can get lost in a fog and your stable footing can start to stumble. With all the pressure of life, our unstable footing while walking in a dense fog with little to no direction created a place that became slippery underfoot for our family.

At this time, Thad and I had been married for over two and a half years and our second son was about to be born. We had done enough small construction jobs to keep our heads above water, but my father-in-law was always afraid to do another house because we still hadn't sold the first spec home. However, Thad was still feeling overwhelmed by the mortgage, the growing family, and the pressure from his father. I didn't know how to help. In reflection, I was hoping that I could lift and ease some of the burden of having a family, a business, and a mortgage at a young age, but I didn't know how other than to pray and hope that he would feel of the strength.

One night my eyes gently fluttered open and reached over to the warmth of the bed for Thad. I felt for him in the soft blanket in the darkness, but he wasn't there. Feeling only cold emptiness, I sat up, look about the room, and saw his silhouette looking out the bedroom window. He was motionless; his figure was fixated on what was beyond the glass pane. I tenderly walked up to him sliding my hand across his back and around his tummy I hugged him from behind allowing my baby bump to rest against him.

I whispered to him "what are you doing? What are you looking at?" He sighed then spoke softly rubbing my arm, "can you hear it?" I was perplexed. *Hear what* I thought? Then he asked again, "can you hear it?" Again, perplexed I looked through the black pane into the darkness and could see or hear nothing. "There's a party. A real party, I wish…" But he stopped his thought like a shadow stretching from a dark corner. He slowly pulled free from my embrace and grasped the casing around the window. The white-knuckled grasp

> *But he stopped his thought like a shadow stretching from a dark corner.*

45

seemed to nearly warp the wood with his force. He stood staring out the window in silence. He was captured by it, and I was captured by his silence and stood frozen in it.

After some time, Thad's question shattered the long silence. He asked me if I could smell "it." "It?", I thought? I sniffed and pulled in a faint whiff of smoke rising in the air like a shadow from the past. "Yes," I replied. More silence. I was trying to figure out what he was wanting. He just stood there and looked through the clear dark glass pane of the window, longing for the party that was out there. He wanted that; he was longing for that party. I reached out again for him, to give him comfort, but he did not respond. He was rooted to the spot; his demon shadow from his past had been awakened. He had no desire to move away from the window. I slowly crept back to bed, and he stood there until I drifted off to sleep again.

The Party—that is what I called it; that was a pivot point for Thad. His longing to be out there with the party instead of with our family was a warning to me. Thad had just given a cry for help, and I should have continued the conversation from that night to the next morning, but I didn't. I just thought it was a strange thing and did not want to really face what was coming.

Thad's longing to be a part of that party was going to come sooner than I thought. I could not believe it. I could not accept that he was going to turn back to that world of addiction. I could not be a part of that world. I didn't understand it. To me the idea of doing drugs, drinking, and longing after it was so foreign. Hadn't Thad already give up all of those things? All I could think of was, "why return to the high school ways to cope with life?" I had no understanding of how to support or help someone that was crying out for help like that other than to pray and hope and to keep on denying what I was about to face.

I was dead wrong. I did *not* understand Thad's stress and coping skills had led him to be an addict once before. The desire and drive of that addiction needed to be fought every day to keep that temptation at bay. I thought that was why we had weekly temple attendance during our first year of marriage— and maybe it was. But we had not been going to the temple together now in about a year. We were not doing what Thad promised would help to keep Satan—the destroyer, at bay.

For my responsibility, I had married someone that had this deep dark history. I knew it was a risk that I took. I simply thought that if we kept to the temple, and if I offered more love, or took away more of the stress, or helped out more, that he would turn back to doing well. I foolishly thought it was that simple. Again, it was not to be. The symbolic Monster of Addiction had been released that night like a shadow, with Thad staring out the window wanting the party. Its fiery breath had melted the foundation we were standing on.

Symbolically, Thad lowered his sword and no longer fought the beast of addiction. The beast had already ensnared him by welcoming him back with open clawed wings. I did not accept this! I struck and struck and hacked at this beast with my might, but Thad was already enveloped in its own dark claws. I could not pry open those wings and I was knocked off my footing.

My world was starting to slide in to more degrees of darkness for me. I felt like I had hit a hard ledge—the very edge of the cliff. Suddenly I heard a momentous crashing sound; I turned to look in the graying darkness just in time to see an avalanche of life tumbling towards my two children and me. We were going to be struck, and little did I know at the time that there would be more victims from this landslide into the darkness of addiction. The beast, the avalanche, the landside all hit to bring us down into the darkness.

# CHAPTER 10

# Addiction: Shackled in pain-filled Comfort

Sliding from the world of light—being sober—in to a world of darkness—addiction—was happening right before my eyes. Despite that, on the last Saturday night in October, a pinpoint of light shone for our family. Our second child was born to us. We named him Garrett. He was named after a missionary we both knew. Thad was there physically and mentally for the birth of his second son, but spiritually, the pull back towards addiction had already begun.

The long cold hard winter was upon us and Thad kept going from job to job and tried to keep the business up. The business was becoming a battleground between both of us because it took so much time, effort, and nearly every conversation was only focused on that.

Soon, old high school friends started coming over and "helping" Thad to do his work. They would all go in to the garage and talk, plan, "think", but I never really saw any work. The planning, the long nights, and putting the business together Thad claimed were happening every night were simply not true.

The cold fingers of winter were finding their way through the glass panes, feeling their way towards my neck as I snuggled down even further in to my bed, my empty bed. Finally, I could take it no longer and I popped my head out of the covers and glanced across the empty side of the bed and at the clock, 2:00 am.

Suddenly I heard banging on the garage door. That must be Thad, I thought. I braced myself and threw off the covers. I quickly plunged my arms in to my robe and wrapped myself in soft warmth. I ran through the carpeted hallway and through the cold laminate kitchen flooring to the door and flew the garage door opened.

Instantly, the icy cold bit at my cheeks and the smell of vomit hit my throat and burned my nose. I flung my arm up to my mouth to protect my breathing and to get through the smell. I looked for the cause of the smell. There it was; the puddle of sick and my husbands passed out hungover body in the wheelbarrow. His head lay to the side of the cold dirty metal with his mouth partially drawn open and heavy breathing of steady steam was escaping his mouth. I was looking at something that would have been in a movie scene, not in my own garage.

The icy cold of the garage started to bite at my bare feet and finger its way through my robe. I found a construction blanket for concrete in the corner of the garage and threw it over Thad's drunken body. I looked back down at him in hot anger—burning red-hot anger. The "scorch the earth" kind of anger welled up inside of me. I had no

*I looked back down at him in hot anger—burning red-hot anger. The "scorch the earth" kind of anger welled up inside of me. I had no words. I had nothing but anger!*

words. I had nothing but anger! I was becoming enraged. I had no compassion for his passed out wasted body in that cold garage. I had no comfort towards him. All I had was hot steely anger. I turned and walked up the four wooden steps in to the house and shut the door. I just left him passed out on the garage, and I returned to the bedroom and sobbed.

What hit me next was a wave of grief that tumbled over me and consumed my heart. The grief caused my heart to shatter! This was a very real moment for me. All I wanted was to have a trusting and loving friend to be married to and to work through our problems together. I had given my trust, my body, and my all to him. We had made covenants to love God and to love each other. Everything I had wanted in my life, all the trust in me, I felt at that moment had been shattered and based on a lie because Thad was wrapped in numbing comfort that became his shackle.

All the trust in our relationship had been stripped from me based on his choices. I was in unfamiliar territory, and I could not see an answer, a goal, or a solution at that moment. I just grieved for what I thought I had. I stayed in those dark pitiful thoughts all through the night. The thought that went through my head over and over was, "we've only been married two and half years. Is life so bad that now we have to drink to get away from our problems?"

As someone so young, naive, and inexperienced about addiction, I didn't know how to truly love Thad or help him as he fell back in to the grasp of drugs and alcohol. I did what I thought was best: I tried harder in pushing him towards love, toward seeing us—towards seeing the family. I wanted him to see us, to feel us, to love us. I thought that the power of love would overcome his addiction. I was right in that the power of love can do that, but it is God's Love. It's His power, not mine that truly heals people.

When I tried to do it with just my love; I was wrong. What I didn't know was that addiction was an illness that must be fought off every minute, every hour, and every day of the addict's life. Thad's pull to turn back towards a place of numbing comfort and to escape the pain of his reality made sense to him. It was not a bad thing in his mind. For him, addiction meant freedom from reality—even if that was for a few moments. He had made that choice.

I tried to paint addiction in to a black and white decision: He had chosen drugs and alcohol, not us. I had no understanding of the POWER that addiction has on its victims. Yes, ultimately addicts make the choice to puff, smoke, drag, swallow, or shoot, however, what pain and addiction that follows after that *first choice* turned out to be out of their hands.

All I hoped for was that I could love him back. Wasn't that what you should do? Yes, I should love him, but part of that is getting help. Getting real help, sharing with others that you need help, but only if the victim has hit bottom or is faced with a decision that is absolute, can addicts start in to recovery. I was too embarrassed to ask for that kind of help. All I could understand was that Thad had walked away from this life once before, and maybe he could do it again. But after more months passed he was not asking for help, but he was embracing the escape again. I was desperately grabbing on to any truth or anything familiar that I could.

What do you do when you are thinking that your life is falling apart? I did one thing right and one thing wrong. Right: I began to pray and pray. My prayers were for the Lord to strengthen Thad so that he would get past the temptations: the drinking, the drugs, and the pornography, and turn to us. I prayed for him feel our love; I felt that it would help, wouldn't it? They were all heartfelt prayers and desires, but in my desperation, I was trying to seek a way to "save Thad."

Wrong thing to do: I told no one. I confided in no one. I thought that if I did, then I would be "airing our dirty laundry." No, I would do this alone.

The image in my mind was from my 4th great grandmother Ellen who crossed the plains with her family putting everything they had in a handcart. They pulled that cart over 1300 miles from Iowa to Utah. I would do the same for Thad. I would pick Thad's broken spirit, mind, and body up off the dirty cold ground and put him into my handcart and pull him into the valley. I would not leave him on the frozen plains of addiction. I was not going to lose him. I was not going to lose the idea of having a marriage. There were therapists, AA meetings, programs, something, and we could find and get the help that was needed. This slide was not going to take all of us down forever. He would stop yelling at us, hurting us—if I could help him. I was going to fight through it, for his sake, and for our family's sake.

It wasn't until years later that I began to understand that I could not control anyone but myself, so I was at the mercy of Thad's agency to choose—and that is a bitter two-edged sword. I simply thought, *this slide in addiction was going to have a bottom soon, and then we could rebuild and repair.* That was all I had to cling to was that hope in a swirling blackening storm of despair.

# CHAPTER 11

# Monticello: A Playground for Mental Illness

Warmth and light filled my sister's car as the gentle hum of the engine carried us into the thickly wooded hills of Virginia. We were in Virginia. We had survived a long cold challenging winter. On his dry days, Thad worked and found enough work to sustain his family of four. We had made it to Virginia from the grace of a construction job that paid us in airline miles. With the miles, we had decided to visit my sister and her family who live in Manassas, VA. She had accepted us as guests and had planned a wonderful trip for us.

As the hum of the car continued, I looked over at my seventh-month-old sleeping son and brushed the wisp of hair off his forehead. I glanced up to see the profile of my husband's face looking out the window. The shadows and sunlight from the thickly wooded trees that lined the road fell on his face creating beautiful patterns of light the enveloped him. He could feel my stare and turned and looked back with a smile and a wink.

The black paved road continued to wind and twist its way through the woods until we came to a clearing that opened and a beautiful Manor house stood stretch out from the road hundreds of yards away; Monticello, Thomas Jefferson's home.

As we walked along the grassy knoll and up to the front door of this incredible historical home, something powerful seemed to grip Thad. The history, the feeling of the place— something had stirred in him. His eyes were laser focused on the details of the woodwork, the curvature of the white painted wood as it enclosed an archway, the crown molding as the 45-degree angles met creating a straight line or the perfectly spun wood railings that stood at attention up the staircase.

The masonry; the way the brick had weathered the elements, the way that the brick stood straight and tall and firm, the mortar holding each red brick in to a cradle of strength and dared the elements to try to take it down—all of it was history and fascinating, and Thad was captured by the beauty of it all.

The interior furnishings had delicate yet strength within the curvature of the chairs, tables, and couches. The legs on the tables and chairs all finished with a claw to show strength. It was filled with Queen Anne style furnishings that displayed rich character in his quarters and yet, in the depth of the kitchen were the large farm style tables with beefy solid legs to hold the pounding of veggies chopping, bread kneading, and meat butchering it could handle. Thad's mind was taking photographs of all the details, and then he was adding calculations and measurements to each detail he looked at.

After leaving the home, the tour led us on the vastness of the grounds, the gardens, and the layout of the entire property. Thad continued in his mind's eye to calculate and survey the grounds as the tour guide explained the various plants and variety and age of trees the Thomas Jefferson had planted.

The history and the beauty awed me, but Thad was awed by something deeper; he had fallen into a playground in his mind where he spent the next two hours walking and talking to himself in a pacing pattern on the grounds of Monticello.

From that trip, Thad saw the inspiration of what to do with the business. He saw how the traditional architecture could come back to life, and he felt that he was the builder to bring that style of building back in to popularity.

He was caught up in all aspects of these thoughts, and it was something that was positive and began to distract him from his poor choices. This was in the spring of the year 2000. Thad had something positive to hold on to and this might be the means to which we stepped and climbed back towards life again away from the fighting and the pull of drugs. That was how I saw it, and I clung to that hope!

Thad fell in to a zone; I called the "work zone." He would design house plans, design the entire feeling and flow of the home to look like history on the outside feel roomy on the inside yet felt like home. His style would shatter the trendy boxy-style houses that were so popular in the 1990's. Thad would talk for hours and hours about how this idea would "revolutionize" the home building industry in the Salt Lake Valley.

Upon returning from Monticello, Thad had gained a new business partner. His name was John. John was someone whom Thad could bounce ideas off and help him think through the challenges that inevitably came *John came in to our lives at the right moment.* up with construction. He was someone who helped keep Thad level-headed. John came in to our lives at the right moment. He helped Thad really connect to the architecture and the way the home really flowed. He also helped Thad think about the exterior and how the look of the home should be balanced.

Thad had found someone he trusted to do business with (besides his father) and I was so excited for him! The mood in the home changed. The old high school friends had been cut off and the power of the drugs and drinking had seemingly slipped back in to the past. This was a miracle! The trip had worked because Thad was going on three months free from drugs and alcohol, and now he had a passion and a direction to keep him focused on real goals.

I couldn't help from having a hopeful and happy heart again. We had this positive and amazing three-month course of racing away from the drugs and alcohol. Thad was breaking down many barriers in business and started having more success. He was winning more and more building jobs, and our family was back on track. I knew that he had a focus and a way to accomplish it.

While I was excited that he was fighting off his demons again, what I should have noticed by this third time of getting clean was actually a dangerous cycle: 1) the pull to drink/drugs, 2) he would hit bottom, 3) then the change of his behavior, 4) then he would be dry again, 5) and finally, making progress again. From that progress and excitement, we would find a happily ever after...for a time.

However, like any Cinderella story, the fairy tale would cycle downward and in to the five steps again. I did not want to see the cycle because when behavior changes happened, I felt hopeful! I clung to the hope that true change had happened. This was the cycle of abuse. Destruction, damage, the pain had been inflicted, and then with time and a few behaviors changes, hope begins to build again. However, the cycle would begin again all too soon, and a sunset would be coming to plunge our hope in to darkness once more.

## SECTION 4 CHILLS

# Chill: Watching someone fall in to the shadow of his or her mind is chilling

CHAPTER 12

# Positive: Weakened Foundations can crack under Pressure

Positive. Positive! I looked at both of the testing applicators. Both had the double pink lines on them. Positive! My head lifted from the countertop and I caught a look of myself in the mirror. My tired green eyes stared back at me. Suddenly out of the corner of the mirror came a blurry face. Thad stepped forward in to clear sharp focus and a sheepish grin hung on the stubble chin as his eyes looked at the two testing applicators. Three months of positive light had given us baby number three.

I turned and hugged him. He returned the hug, but it felt stiff; then his hand white-knuckled behind me and pressed in to my back. I was a bit surprised. I struggled and pulled away. I tried to look at his eyes, but he would not look directly at me but passed me. He turned from me and walked towards his drafting table slowly releasing his hand and shaking it as he walked. Soon I heard the slide and scrap of the rulers against the paper and the scratching of the pencil as more house plans fell from his head onto the page.

I leaned against the doorframe and watched him work on the house plans. I turned and went in to the bedroom to finish up a few things. When I returned, I found Thad on the phone talking very animatedly. Thad quickly whispered to me that it was John and that he wanted to see the house plans. Thad continued his conversation with John and then hung up the phone. He said that he would be back—that John wanted to meet him and go over a few things. I told him to invite John here that way Thad could keep working and not get interrupted. Thad just smiled and said that he would be back in a few hours. With that, he was off.

I just smiled, John, good old John. I went back into the bathroom and finished cleaning up the positive tests and picked up my little Garrett and just held him as we danced and swayed in the bathroom. Things were better. Things were good. It was important that I keep a hold of this positive thought and live in the moment of this sunshine. A smile softly split across my face, child number three would be coming in the spring, and with that, I continued to sway and dance with Garrett; his hand flicking as we were watching our reflection in the mirror with hope.

The coolness of that summer morning was nearing its end and the sun began to heat the air. My mind started a running checklist of all that we were doing: Thad was designing house plans, he was back at church, we were getting steady work, the family felt secure and happy and we would be adding one more to it.

However, as the heat of summer slowly turned in to a crisp biting fall, the dew on the surface of our lives turned to frost and ice which caused us to slip and slide off our positive uphill climb away from drugs and alcohol. It was like the power of the ice freezing and thawing, cracking and weakening the foundation. Soon we would find ourselves slipping and sliding on the icy coldness of a relapse and the crack fractured the foundation as Thad had fallen back in to the cold steel grip of addiction and abuse.

*However, as the heat of summer slowly turned in to a crisp biting fall, the dew on the surface of our lives turned to frost and ice which caused us to slip and slide off our positive uphill climb away from drugs and alcohol.*

Why? What had happened? It was simple really; it started with a phone call. An old high school friend called. He needed a ride home from an all-night binge. Thad was pacing up and down in the hallway. He was talking to himself. Sometimes a smile would split across his face and sometimes, a deep grimace. He was in turmoil over this phone call.

I reached out and caught his arm as he passed by me for the fourth time and I begged him not to go. I begged him to let his other friends and family deal with it. Thad stopped. His blue eyes looked directly in to mine. He held my gaze for some time. He took my arm and pulled me in close giving me a hug. I relaxed in to him. He held me there for a few minutes. I felt that he had made his choice to stay and so I raised my head to look in to his eyes and tell him thank you when he suddenly interrupted my thoughts.

He looked at me and told that he was strong. That he was just going to give him a ride home, and then he would return. What could go wrong? He pulled away from my hug, reached for his coat, his keys and he smiled and shut the front door behind him.

I walked to the window and I pulled the curtain aside and watched him drive out to leave behind the red taillights until they faded from view. I sighed...my gut told me this was so wrong. That he was too weak, just too weak, and unfortunately, I was right.

Once again around 3:00 am I reached out and felt the empty cold pillow where his head should be but wasn't. And just like that, the past four months of positive focused work, repentance, family time, and jobs had gone up in a flash of flames and I was left with wisps of smoke to try to grasp on to as they dissipated through my fingers. Positive? What was positive?

# CHAPTER 13

# Thad Land: A Funhouse or a Madhouse?

If you have ever been inside a Funhouse when you were younger? You probably experienced fun surprises like a spinning tunnel, blasts of air as you tried to manipulate obstacle courses or trick mirrors that distort the truth of what you are seeing. In many cases, it's just fun to see those comparisons and experience the oddities of the house. You usually leave laughing and have fun stories to tell about it to your friends. However, have you ever experienced a Madhouse? What is the difference? It is the same types of tunnels, obstacle courses, and mirrors distorting the truth now mixed with psychosis and a feeling that you will never find an escape.

Idaho was like a bright flash of flame that left us as a burnt cinder in our lives. Flash of flame: 1) we left the old friends behind, 2) Thad had a job, and 3) we had been blessed to find a home. For the first few weeks, it was wonderful. Thad would leave for work on time and actually return home. The first payday we had, I celebrated! I was so thrilled for him. I embraced him and gave him a huge kiss letting him know that I was very proud of him.

However, Thad shook off my kiss and my hug and returned it with a smirked. His response threw me off base. I looked at him and could not understand why. He became really quiet and just kept smirking. He had a look of intensity that came over him. Then he blurted out something I will never forget. He said that he was "owned by someone." He said, "I am a slave!" I didn't understand. *Owned by someone—a slave?* I thought?

He said that he was a businessman; that he had a business. He repeated, "I have my *own* business." Then under his breath, I heard, "I am Thomas!" I looked at him and his whisper face changed instantly back to shouting that now he was owned. My eyes bounced around his pain-filled face as I tried to see what had happened. He just kept screaming how he hated this. He said, "I was supposed to be in charge—the boss—the one calling the shots." But now? Now? Now, he was just a slave? A slave to the big man, a slave to what the boss wanted him to do.

His shouts trailed off like an echo bouncing off the kitchen. Suddenly another sharp whisper, "I am Thomas!" escaped his pursed tighten lips. My breath caught. I heard that very clear. I looked at him; he dropped his head, and then suddenly raised it. "I have no more freedom. I have no more worth." Then with rounded shoulders and head bend down, he said, "I am just a slave."

I stood in the moment of that communication outburst feeling as if a knife had slashed me. I thought to myself: a slave? Not a boss? Thomas? Did he mean Thomas Jefferson? Not one of his slaves? What? A slave?—We had an income. That was stability, not slavery. I heard those words fly out of his mouth, but I didn't know how to respond. For me, I thought that having a boss meant that I didn't have to do the books; that I didn't have to hound people for money to pay

Thad. All the business stress was over for me since he went to work for someone. I thought that he would put in his time at work, and then on his own, he could still create his business.

I just sat there on the kitchen chair with no response. I had just been blown over. My face showed it and Thad with the same smirk got up and walked out slamming the kitchen door. The intense moment between us had set off Garrett in a shrieking rage. My three-month-old whom I held in my arms, wanted to nurse, and Kellis returned to the kitchen telling me that he was hungry.

As Garrett started to calm down, my mind started thinking. "Ok, I could see Thad's perspective: many people would rather be the boss then the grunt." What does he mean? He IS Tomas Jefferson? No, no—he is Thad, not Thomas Jefferson. But what I wasn't seeing was the two worlds that Thad was living in: the "Thad Land" of his mind, and the other of his married/family life. Out of the two worlds—I had to break in to this world of "Thad Land" soon. I had to figure out how he thought, why he thought this way; our family's future depended on it.

Day after day, we would wake with blue haze outside in the cool morning. The haze was soon penetrated by the soft glow of the sun, then it would dissipate, and it would turn in to the heat of the day. Our lives continued day-by-day set at this pace. I praised Thad for all that he was doing: we were employed and had a steady income. He was leaving in the morning for work and coming home at night. With this positive light, we also received great news that the Spec home was finally under contract and sold two days later for a cash offer.

I took my children with me to Utah to close on the home, spend time with family, and then returned to Idaho. I could feel us leaving the light behind. I felt like I was driving in to

65

a gray storm that was neither light nor dark. As we got closer and closer all I could feel was a pang that something was off. I would soon learn of that reality—of what had been happening in Idaho while we were gone. Soon the gray storm would set in on us and would melt in to a black nightmare.

Thad's mom had decided to come up to Idaho with us to see her son for a few days. She drove her car and we traveled caravan style. I was really excited for Carla to see Thad in a great place. Maybe she would see him sober other than drunk or hungover. Our drive from Utah to Idaho was uneventful, but the hours that followed would be filled with the knowledge of events that would break me to the core of my beliefs, and my reality in my carefree land of Idaho would melt soon vanish.

I grasped the metal handle of the front door and twisted, turned and pushed the heavy door open. I entered within the walls of our rental house a clean, organized, beautiful sunlit entryway. It caught my breath and I was in shock. Thad was there with a huge hug and a kiss and welcomed us all in. The kids went running from room to room and shouted, "Clean, clean, clean." My relief and happiness seemed to glow on my face.

After getting settled back into a routine, Thad wanted to take his mom for a drive. I thought that that would be great. After all, I had been able to spend nearly two weeks with her, and I didn't want to hog her anymore. After they left, I looked at the entire house. Everything was in its place; everything was over the top organized. I found myself in the basement getting a toy for Isaac when I noticed something was wrong. It wasn't a physical object, but it was more like a feeling was out of place. I felt a dark shadow behind me. It was very eerie, and I bolted up the stairs scared of the feeling.

Within a moment of me noticing the feeling, Garrett sensed something as well. He began to shriek and scream as if a scorpion had stung him. I could not settle him down. He thrashed about and was struggling to find peace. I could not understand what had set him off. He could not adjust to being home. My two other children waited for me and kept them busy while I worked with Garrett. It took about two hours for Garrett to exhaust himself until he finally collapsed asleep.

Suddenly it was dinnertime, and then clean up, then tub time and soon the difficulty with sleeping came over us. I began to feel a sickness in the depth of my stomach. I did not know what was wrong, but there was something going on. Where were Thad and Carla?

Thad and his mom arrived home late well after midnight. Carla looked worn out, more than just tired; literally worn out. She excused herself and headed downstairs to go to sleep. Thad looked a little sheepish and gave me a halfhearted hug. I wanted to embrace him, to make this sickness go away. I wanted to feel love, feel proud of him; I wanted to be with him. We walked to the bedroom to finally be together. I tried to let my needs known to him, but he just rolled over and fell asleep. I was a little hurt and confused, I just left it at that and collapsed in to sleep myself.

The following day Carla was tired again, and very emotional. I was trying to figure out what was going on. She would just pick up one of the grandkids and hold them or busy herself with them. I asked Thad why wasn't he going to work? He just said that he was too tired and left. I was lost in too many unsaid thoughts to understand what was even going on.

I caught Carla crying and crying after lunch. I asked her what was wrong? She just shook her head and said that she was just emotional. She quickly changed the subject and began reading to Kellis. She played and read and laughed and held the children. She kept herself busy all afternoon while I tried to figure out what was happening, and why I was feeling that something was so wrong.

Soon Thad came home and found me talking to Carla. I was trying to understand what had happened on the car ride when Thad suddenly blurted out "I *slept* with someone while you were gone!"

It was like time was suspended with his words. They hung in the air like a dark echo bouncing around in a black cave. That sentence, "I slept with someone", was like a sledgehammer of truth shattering against the clean fake facade that Thad had created. Suddenly, those words returned like a boomerang and came pounding into my head and heart. What?? I kept repeating that over and over. What?? The confusion, the mountain of pain, the shock! What??

> *That sentence, "I slept with someone", was like a sledgehammer of truth shattering against the clean fake facade that Thad had created.*

Suddenly I was enraged, and I lit into Thad. I was shouting, screaming, and my yelling set off a firestorm of screams from Garrett! I felt the hot blistering anger rise up my face! Images of a faceless woman in my bed holding onto the man I was married to seared in to my mind's eye. I gasped for air and felt out of breath. My heart was racing. My head was pounding, hot anger leaked from my eyes, and my panic shifted in to trying to find an answer, a resolution, and a place of peace.

Shattered—our world we had been trying to piece together glass fragment by glass fragment with my bloodstains on the sharp edges was no longer even in existence. I was shattered. Broken. Annihilated. I felt cheap, like a floozy. Worthless. Empty. Nothing!

I was a fool! I thought that Thad and I were back on track. I had felt hope. I had felt light again. But now, it was as if the evil shadows from the four corners of a room raced with shrill laughter and mocking fingers towards my small pinpoint of light I had been holding and snuffed it out.

It was a firestorm of words that led to me being chard like cinders and ashes. It also led to Thad's first physical blow against my face, back, and arm. I was hurt, I struck out to fight back and lost.

Carla left the next day, and I tried to assess the damage to our family. Do I kick him out? Do we leave Idaho and return to Utah—but where? Back to the basement—where? From August to the beginning of September all I could do was live hour by hour locked in a deep pit of despair and grief for our marriage. In my grief over the marriage, I did not see the depth of Thad's mind and mental health had been altered. I would see him pace and walk and talk to himself. I would also see him stare expressionless in to space for hours. It took him days to make simple decisions. His skill set and focus was plummeting and soon work began to fall by the wayside, and the pains of stress, hunger, and hanging by our fingernails returned.

I tried in vain I tried to reach John. I needed to tell him about how Thad keeps calling himself Thomas Jefferson. How Thad can't plan, can't create, and keeps drinking and drinking. I kept trying to call John, but all the numbers that Thad had ever given me had been changed. Thad said that he and John had gotten in to a fight while I was in Utah and to never contact him again. Thad was in charge—not John! John was nothing to him anymore. That John's business ideas were junk and that only he really knew how to build. Thad's mental abilities to cope with all were happening was getting worse.

I found myself in the darkness of a cold empty bed fading in and out of sleep and reality. Suddenly my hand stretched and reached toward the doorknob. My fingers were so close to touching it. The doorknob was covered in words, and I was close enough that could almost read them. Stretch! I commanded myself. Reach! You must open that door! Suddenly like a hot fire, I felt the shrieking screams of someone in absolute pain! My eyes flew awake. A dream! A dream! I was only in a dream. However, the screaming never stopped! I shook myself and was released from my dream. It was Garrett. I threw off the covers and ran toward his room.

I gasped and caught my breath as I peeked through the doorway. Thad was standing there staring at Garrett. He had a white-knuckle grip on his crib, and his face was red with rage. He was spewing hurtful evil words at this child. "I'm Thomas!" He hissed. "I am free!" He hissed again. "You are the slave! I own you!" His voice was gaining strength, "You can NEVER take my freedom!" I was trying to figure out how to grab Garrett. I needed to distract Thad. "Oh, God!" I prayed, "Please help me!" I felt prompted to use my phone. I ran as softly as I could back to the room and grabbed it.

I dialed the number and left it on the bed and ran back to the room. He was startled and shaken from his dialog. He turned and grabbed his phone. At that same moment, I slipped in and reached to the side of the crib and grabbed Garrett and ran! I had saved him from Thad's staring eyes and dark words.

I ran from the room, Thad raced after me and slammed against the door, but the door held firm. Garrett's shrieks and cries continued with me on the other side of that door. Thad slammed against the door a few more times shouting, "He does not own me! I am the boss! He can't take away my freedom!" There were two more lunges at the door, then silence. I still held my hands firmly against the door until I heard the bathroom door slam shut, the lock click, and the water started running.

I released my hands from the door leaving moistened handprints behind. I quietly opened the door. I ran back to the room and grabbed Kellis and Isaac. I quickly locked the door behind me, and I tucked them in to my bed. I walked, swayed, and held Garrett and continued to pray through the night for our safety. My prayer would be interrupted by a hissing

> *I released my hands from the door leaving moistened handprints behind.*

sound of Thad whispering "freedom" at random moments through the door. I only had a flimsy lock between Thad and me. Thad kept whispering through the long night. I kept rocking and holding Garrett helping to calm his crying to whimpering to finally silence. I finally joined my other boys in the bed and collapsed until the morning.

As the warm rays of sunrise filtered into the room, I shot awake. It took me a minute to recognize why I had everyone in the bed with me and then the sinking feeling of last night began to overshadow me. I left the comfort of the bed and began to dress for the day. Soon, because of my movement, my children were also awake. I unlocked the door and looked around to see if Thad was there. I looked out the front window and the truck was gone. My tense shoulders relaxed. I went back into the room and brought out everyone to start breakfast. After a few quick bites, I went out to the living room and turned on the TV.

Suddenly at that very moment, the images that I saw were that of another nightmare. I could hear shrieking and gasping as the images of a plane plowing into a tower on the TV unfolded in front of my eyes. It was like an out of body experience was happening to me—I was the one gasping and screaming. The spiral in to darkness was happening, and my life was out of control. My children stared at me as they saw me enter my screams of terror that September 11th morning.

My eyes never left the TV screen. The fire, the smoke, the building, the questions, then as some answers started to come together I witnessed the second plane smashing into the second tower! My tears running over my red, hot cheeks seemed to carve perfect tracks down my face. I blew out billowy fiery breaths and inhaled deeply to stoke the grief, devastation, and hurt of 9/11.

After a few hours of watching it, Thad came back to the house. He entered the living room and stood behind me watching the play by play of that dark September morning. I turned around to Thad and said, "I am going home." His blank eyes just stared past me. I turned back to the screen. I was determined to find a way to get the children back home. Thad started to whisper about getting his freedom again—that he would be free soon. He stood and walked towards the door and quickly shot a look back to me as the shadow fell across his face. "Thomas is right. John will never know", were his words as he stepped through the door. He was lost in his Thad Land.

I tossed the last black bag full of clothes on top of the furniture heap, grasped hold of the rope, jumped from the back of the moving truck, onto the frozen street. As I jumped I pulled the door down with a hard slam! I cranked the metal hook to lock it shut. I crunched on the ice around to the side of the truck and thumped on the door. Thad fired up the rented truck and slowly put it in to gear. I walked to the blue paint-pealing car, waved to my three buckled inside and sat in the seat.

I held the steering wheel as I cranked the starter until it caught. I pulled the gearshift in to drive and rolled away. I felt the weight of it all slamming in to me as mile after mile I slid in to more and more darkness. It was just like following the sickly red lights from the rental truck—darkness was engulfing me.

What had I learned in Idaho? 1) I was weak, unloved, and unwanted. 2) Thad had intense mind problems. 3) I needed to run away from the hellish nightmare in Idaho. I was a chard and broken; a burnt cinder because of the adultery, the abuse, and the intense needs of my children. I had no light to cast before my path but for the sickly red lights on the moving truck.

CHAPTER 14

# A Beautiful Mind: Finding John

Minds: imagination, thinking, dreaming, organizing, logic; minds are wonderful. They can lead us to wonderful places. All that is creative comes from some type of inspiration, and it helps to deepen the experience of life. We are all encompassed about with intelligence, our own thoughts, and thinking about what other people think of us. Minds are amazing when they are healthy, but if illness flows in, the pain is more than anything physical. It is all-consuming.

The movie *A Beautiful Mind* is a journey that takes the viewer on a ride of a mental fright, after all, it is based on a true story. The main character, John Nash, has a brilliant yet, sick mind. Although John's mind can mathematically understand the reality of numbers and economics, it also splits in to a non-reality; for him it is very real. His mind developed characters that were never "real" in the physical sense, but always real to him. They were his friends, his companions.

They taught him, laughed with him, and comforted him just as any real friends do. Later, however, they confused him, teased him, and pulled him from the reality that he thought he was living and in to a world that he was so convinced was real that there was no boundary between non-reality and reality.

The confusion of what *was* real and what was *not* real became the next challenge in my life during the last five years of my marriage. Our Beautiful Mind journey began during the Thad Land experience in Idaho. There had been clues that things were not right with Thad's mental health: long conversations with himself, odd irrational behavior, confusion of his identity (calling himself Thomas Jefferson), and paranoia.

Thad had one topic of conversation that consumed him. *Revolutionary Homes*: the construction and building of houses. Thad's mind had hundreds of different house plans. He had a gift. He was to wood, as Michelangelo was to marble. He was going to "revolutionize the building industry" because of his architecture and building ideas.

He was going to give his homes a variety of colors, textures, and open floor plans/living spaces. On the outside, the homes would range from the bungalow, ranch style, craftsman, stick build, Dutch colonial, and have a flare of Queen Anne/ Victorian with different exterior colors, and building materials. He was going to draw, design, and construct these homes by himself with his two friends. The homes would change the landscape and entire subdivisions! These homes would become the most sought after homes. These would become a revolution in itself. These types of homes would become, *Revolutionary Homes*.

But one night, after intense work on Revolutionary Homes, he said he wanted to watch something and just chill out. I popped in a DVD we hadn't watched yet. We watched *A Beautiful Mind*.

As the movie unfolded, I watched the movie with a sickening fascination; and that disturbed me. As the scenes fell before me, I was captivated by the main character and how he became so involved in the non-reality of his mind. I was enraptured as I watched the main character converse, argue, and enjoy his "non-reality" friends. I was spellbound. The depth of the character's illusions was fierce and powerful because his intelligence did not distinct his "friends" from reality or imaginary.

My heart then began to break for the main character, John, because he had to fight to remember to divide the reality from imagination every day. The movie portrayed that battle as being exhausting. I felt heartbroken for his wife who had to guess and identify when he has in and out of reality. She had to ultimately learn how to trust when John was in reality, and when he was drowning in his other world. I was amazed at how they figured out a way to live a semi-normal life—at least according to how the movie portrayed it.

Tears were streaming down my face and my heart felt like it was in an emotional press as I continued to watch. All I could do was to sit and let the tears slip silently down my face as the credits scrolled up across the TV screen. My thoughts continued going over and over again in my head about the main character, John, and his daily mental battle. It was just fascinating.

Thad had been sitting on the couch, with his face still facing the TV. He hadn't moved the entire movie. In fact, I had forgotten we had watched it together. As the last of the credits disappeared and the music faded, Thad turned to me and said forcefully, "Finally!" Minutes then seem to slowly tick by, and then he said with relief, "someone understands the way I think!"

Thad had a look of relief and excitement and he kept on smiling and chuckling to himself. I sat

*"Finally!" Minutes then seem to slowly tick by, and then he said with relief, "someone understands the way I think!"*

there stunned and in disbelief. Wait... What?? At first, my mind was just swirling and repeated his exclamation, "finally someone understands the way I think?!" It swirled for a few minutes more. What was Thad saying? Then suddenly my mind seemed to connect the images and feelings over the past five years of marriage.

No words came out of my mouth. My mouth hung wide open. I just sat there. My mind broke in to hundreds of images of Thad talking to himself, his drive times, and his odd conversations with clients about how his company would revolutionize the home building industry. I immediately thought about the list of friends that he had. I thought about the friends and people the main character interacted with in such a real way but were only people of his mind. Suddenly the comparison of John Nash and Thad were starting to melt together in my mind. I could see the similarities: loner, paranoid, brilliant, consumed in his mind every waking hour by the business.

My heart and thoughts began to race as my mind replayed those images again and again. "Someone understands the way I think." I looked at Thad and again, he had a look of relief on his face. He simply said that he could finally tell people how he thinks: that he has "strings of thoughts" just like the main character. "Someone understands the way I think."

My mind was screaming, "strings of thoughts...understands the way I think?" Was Thad referring to the way the character solves problems by seeing patterns in print, commercials, and so forth to find answers, OR was he talking about his friends—*mind friends*? He was talking about both.

Thad was just so happy to have answers. He said that his friend, John, understood him the same way. Then all at once Thad fell in to his own world and just walked away from me. I was just stunned and sat on the couch trying to process what had happened. I was still lost in the emotion of the movie and then the words that Thad had said to me were crashing over me like a waterfall. I was trying to fight my way through the pounding waves of emotion and the words that Thad had said to me. I was trying to understand what my current reality was.

My mind then flashed to John—Thad's business partner. The one I could *never* reach by phone, but Thad always could. John, the one that gave him all the advice. John, who had left for a period of time when we moved to Idaho, but then returned when we came back to Utah. John, the one I never spoke with or never met. The one that was *only* there for Thad—he was a *mind friend*! John was never real! Thomas Jefferson! Who was that? Thad would refer to himself as Thomas when he felt threatened that he was losing his freedom! That he was never going to be owned! These were his *mind friends*!

I didn't know what to think or to feel with this newly discovered level of insanity! I would panic, or zone out, or cry as my thoughts continued to swirl around me. I had a choice to make on this new path. I could pray for Thad and hope that he would maintain control of himself while I looked for support and help in a way that wouldn't scare Thad, and that would help us to survive. I needed to find mental stability. I needed to find a way to provide for the family, but this was an added stress that would guarantee that my full-time job was going to be for the safety of my children.

I needed to keep sane myself. I had to watch for clues of Thad's *mind friends*: I kept my eye out for John and for when Thad would refer to himself as Thomas. I had to see some tangible evidence of both characters so that I could get Thad some help. I was watching and documenting when and why Thad would become these people. This was the direction that I choose—to would try and get Thad help. I felt that was towards the light and hopefully would brighten my darkening storm of life that surrounded me.

CHAPTER 15

# The Red House:
# The Cherry Days

"One more house" said John, "then you will have revolutionized the home building in America." Thad looked over the farmland about to be plowed under for pipes, utilities, roads, and homes. His breath seemed to hang in the air like a frosty cloud. John sat next to him in the truck with his outstretched hand pointing across the landscape.

Together, two men in faded jeans, work boots, and layered hoodies looked out over the fields. The sky had a paint stroke of pale pink in the gray in the cold sunset. The dense fog clouds were rolling in from off the Great Salt Lake. John kept talking about drawing 30 different house plans, and mixing and matching the colors, the textures, and giving the country the homes that the people wanted." This is how Thad saw his business meeting with John. If anyone else saw it, it would look like a lone man, looking at a field, and talking to himself. This is what I saw as I walked up to the truck to bring him his dinner.

Thad had one topic of conversation with John: *Revolutionary Homes*. He would talk about some amazing ideas of how to capture turn of the century architecture and break the trend of boxy hip roof homes. Thad knew where he wanted to build homes like this and that he could then enter the Parade of Homes. All the builders competed to get in to the Parade of Homes because it showed off your skills and style. The public got hooked on the looks and feels, and the builders got more and more build jobs. Thad was convinced that the entire Valley was now going to want his *Revolutionary Homes*. The home to start this change was called the Red House.

I wanted to figure out a way to love and trust Thad again. I wanted to give one more shot at saving the marriage. I thought that if we could work together physically and emotionally building a new house side by side maybe he would start to cleave to me and none else. I felt that we might recreate what we had done when we were engaged—build something together. I would forgive the times he yelled, neglected us, drank, did drugs, hit/grabbed us. I would even tolerate his conversations about John, if we could reclaim our love we had during our first two years. So, we sank all of our money and our in-law's money in to building the *Revolutionary Home*. We broke ground in September 2002 on the *Red House* in Huntsville.

> *I felt that we might recreate what we had done when we were engaged—build something together.*

Side by side Thad and I worked together to cut down on the costs of building this huge 5,000 sq. foot home. Thad and I surveyed the lot, excavated, dug footings, set concrete forms, poured the foundation, did the cement work, laid the floor cap, and framed the house together. The work that Thad and I did on the house was bringing us together. We worked through all sorts of weather: hail, sleet, rain, and the winter snows. Together, we were physically building the home from September 2002 to March 2003.

There were moments of magic, months of soberness, and moments of true love. The months of soberness brought our family closer together. Thad attended church with the family, and I was feeling a sense of peace and love again. The *Red House* really was helping us to rebuild our trust as a couple again. Thad would actually invest back in the relationship by asking how the children were doing. He was gaining some interest in wanted to help them, and to help me. It was a time that I could breathe, build trust, and have moments of hope and love enter back in to my heart.

The love, trust, and moments soon brought news of a fourth child. Our lives were rebuilding, our relationship was mending because we were building it together. There were five to six months of peace: of Thad being home at night and the family healing. Thad never displayed his *mind friends* to me during this time. He talked about the business within "normal ranges."

I hand scraped the tongue and groove of over 5000 square feet of one and a quarter inch thick hard maple floors the spring of 2003 as my last supportive efforts towards to the home. Those floors came from the old Indian school in Brigham City. Thad and his dad pulled out those floors to help save costs for the home. I had physically reached everything I could with the home because my belly was rounding out again for the fourth time.

The exterior was complete: walls up, a wraparound porch with fifteen pillars, metal roof, copper hood for the fireplace, deep Cherry Red color Masonite siding, and soft white trim, casings, and trim work throughout the exterior. On the interior: heavy glass doors for the dining room, twelve built-in custom cabinets, the finished maple flooring throughout the main floor, the mother-in-law apartment over the garage, the upstairs master suite, the stairs, and hallways.

The colors reflected the character of the farm style and the crispness of the modern day all in one. The white kitchen, granite countertops, and pop of apple green paint color against the white and the maple really made a statement. The miles of trim work, bead-board, and casings made the home very custom and something that could never be duplicated. The full finished basement contained a large entertainment room, another bedroom, two large storage rooms, and a cool little nook and playhouse under the stairs.

The Red House was on schedule to be completed in October 2003. Through the building of the Red house, more people were indeed noticing the fine textures, the style, the woodwork, the layout of the home and everything that Thad had said would attract them to Revolutionary Homes.

Two very interested parties who saw the construction of the Red House came directly to Thad: 1) my parents and 2) an investor who wanted a home to be built in the Parade of Homes. That investor home must be completed by the spring of 2004. Soon the contracts lay before us followed by the scratching sound of pen on paper. Two contracts were ready to go, so the digging began!

My parents had decided to build a dream home close to our home in the mountain valley of Huntsville. They wanted a farm style home with a full basement. Thad was able to place the home on the lot, which gave it views of the valley, an open walkout basement, and space between neighbors. It was bright and yellow and filled with hope. The construction of that house helped to support our income, and it was building my parents a home of their lifetime.

Thad also had a client that wanted her home to be in the Parade of Homes. We did not have to have the financial risk of a spec home because we had a paying client! She wanted a Craftsman/Bungalow style home that had all the details and design that Thad specialized in. The home was to be featured in a revitalize Ogden project, and it would be the featured home of the parade. It was a dream come true for Thad, and for us!

The Red House was a slice of time to rebuild my strength in my family, my faith, and in our marriage. The cherry days were a challenge because they played with my mind: filled with hope, sober again, changed behavior, no fights, home on time, reminding me why I loved him. Those months were a huge blessing and strength to me, then again there was a small part of me reminding me to see the cycle again—it had been the pattern that after something so worthwhile, the fall would soon come. The cherry days teased me. It was a mind game. It was a reprieve from the darkness, but soon the darkness would engulf us again.

# CHAPTER 16

## Scattered Pieces: Will the Pieces Fit?

L eft foot: lift, flex, reach, and step. Now repeat with your right foot: lift, flex, reach and step. Just keep walking. Push the stroller with your arms and keep stepping—that's it. Let the wheels roll out in front of you and keep walking, keep going. You need to get to the car and get home, my thoughts were telling me. I stood in a sea of cars in the parking lot. My eyes stretched out across the various colors and shapes until I saw the van. My head continued to encourage me, "You are almost there. Keep walking. Keep going…." But I was like an echo of silence—not heard.

With each step I began to gain a small amount of feeling. I asked myself, "How did I get here in this parking lot?" Then the memory of four weeks ago flooded my mind. The four walls, the table, a sink and spinney stool of the doctor's office and the four walls met in to four perfect corners, and Garrett was lining the cars up along the south wall. The dark, soft eyes set behind a pair of black rimmed glasses of my pediatrician was reading through the answers I had given to the questions on the yellow form. Occasionally, he would lift his eyes from the page and watch my child "play" with different sets of toys. I kept looking from his eyes to my child and back.

After 40 minutes of questions, answers, and observations, my Pediatrician said to me, "April, I believe your child has autism." Autism? I remember thinking. What is that? He handed me information. It was something about a research project that offered free testing and diagnosis for autism. The research project needed volunteers, following all the testing they could get a diagnosis.

My head was spinning but I could not find any more questions to ask my pediatrician. Dazed by all of this information, I lifted Garrett up off the floor and buckled him in to the stroller. I took the information from his hand and he looked at me with tired sad eyes. I thanked him for his help and pushed the stroller with Garrett out the door. We were transitioning from the doctor's office back to the van and that started the shrieking and screaming all the way to the elevator.

Three weeks after that appointment with my pediatrician; it was time for our day at the autism research project. I was no longer numb; I was ready. I needed answers, so I was ecstatic to get information and results at the beginning of the week. I knew that if Garrett had autism, then I could finally get him the right help. I needed that diagnosis! Every day for one week we made the two-hour drive to the research project. Every day we stayed for a six-hour day of testing, questioning, giving genetic material, MRI's, two-way mirrors, and of answering more questions.

But now, as I coached myself to the car, my emotions could not be identified. I had just left the genetic research center with my three children for the last time that week. I was returning with *three* files full of results from a week worth of testing. *Three* files? I was there for just to find answers for one, for Garrett. I needed answers; a diagnosis, a label so that I could get Garrett services. They needed to test Kellis and Isaac to compare things; but they were typical—right? They were tested just to compare, I kept telling myself. How could I be returning home with two more files? I was supposed to return with answers for Garrett. That testing was only to identify Garrett. I had no idea it had also identified my two other children as being on the autism spectrum.

My mind kept coaching me to get the kids buckled and to drive home. I needed to get home. I felt that angels must have guided me home that day because I can't remember the drive. I pulled the van into the driveway, put the van in park, and opened the door and looked at the three faces of my children. I unclicked, unbuckled, and lifted them through the kitchen door and kicked it shut. I released my three children into the home and pulled from my black bag three files.

All three files slipped from my shaking hands, hitting the kitchen floor of our home, spilling its orderly contents in to a scattered mess. I slid down the wall and onto the hardwood floor with scattered pieces of paper from the files all around me. My eyes jumped from pieces of sentences, to pieces of photos, to bits of words what had been typed by my children's names: autism, low functioning, high functioning, social disconnections, rigid routines, inflexibility, low verbal, high interest, low spontaneity, rapid head growth, infrequent eye contact, and inability to answer social questions. Those words rose off the pages like a wisp of dreams that had turned to smoke never to be realized.

*Those words rose off the pages like a wisp of dreams that had turned to smoke never to be realized.*

My thoughts were triggered by those scattered pieces of words that lifted from the coarse paper by my eyes. The words began a tug of war putting my mind in a set of action, but my emotions just sat in a river of denial. The more my eyes raked of the words more words built the conversation in my head that went something like this: "Garrett was the one that rocked, punched, bit, hit, flapped, and threw tantrums. Garrett was the one with self-injurious behavior, with aggression against others and against objects."

Garrett was the one with poor eye contact. He couldn't use language to communicate—he only cried and screamed. He shut down, he could repeat hours' worth of scripts from movies, but he used no words to have his needs or wants to be met. He bit, he hit, and he screamed. He had night terrors. He was sensitive to lights, sounds, smells, and touch. He lined things up. He would spin the wheels on cars. He clicked, flapped, and hit himself. He had autism. He needed more early intervention. He needed a program. He is on the waiting list for things. He needed to get help!

I read through Kellis's file. Kellis used language—he had a HUGE vocabulary. He loved words. He would use words that kids four years older than him would use. Kellis communicated his needs and wants. Kellis was shy when around others and preferred to be alone but was calm. He was sick with ear infections, strep throat, and extreme eating issues, but he talked. He seemed to only talk about one subject. The pre-school teacher had a few things she was concerned with: He hated to hold pencils in his hand because of the scraping feeling, he could tell the teacher encyclopedia amounts of information about different subjects, and he loved to be with her. He did not interact with the peers around him.

Isaac was a mover—he was wiggly, but he had been since he was in my tummy. He loved to crawl, jump off things, and jump on the trampoline. He hated haircuts. He hated to eat different things but was really quiet and calm when I

compared him to Garrett. He could tolerate Garrett screaming and crying. He communicated with me, I think...well, he
would pull me over to things to get what he needed, but that
was helpful because Garrett was usually in a tantrum, so he
figured out how to compensate or figured a way to communicate with me by pulling me over to his wants and needs.
He said mama, ball, food, milk, jump...but no sentences....
He was nearing three years old.

My numbness crashed over me as I looked again at the
scattered pieces. The words sent a cascade of tears down my
face and I fell in to my own silence. Silence—my head was
finally silent, from all the conversations I had had with it.

My mind had just listed all the reasons why two of my
children did NOT have autism, but why one did. However, I
could see my list of reasons begin to solidify instead of fade. In
the scattered pile at my feet, I reached out and read a piece of
paper. There was a list of reasons why my two other children
were identified. Social disconnections: Kellis disconnected
from peers but was great with adults. Rigid routines: both
liked the routines I had set with Garrett and they would
tantrum if I strayed. Inflexibility: that was true about Kellis
and his food, and Isaac and sharing any toy. Low verbal: this
goes with Isaac; he should be saying three-word sentences
and connecting with others socially. High interest: both loved
Legos. Low spontaneity: they were predictable. This caused
my emotions to run deeper.

Symbolically, I felt like I was drowning in the river of denial
but kept resurfacing. This river trip was short. I had to get off
the river of denial and face the reality of having three children
on the autism spectrum; otherwise, no one would help them.

The sentence from my oldest son's file that stuck with me
said: "Symptoms must be present in early childhood but may
not become fully manifest until social demands exceed limited
capacities." To the right of that sentence was a check mark. He
had other checklists, but that stuck out to me: "until the social

demands exceed limited capacities." Preschool, church settings, and parties: those social demands gave Kellis a different result when compared to peers his age. He would go alone, choose to build something or hang out with the adults. As much as I hated it, that scattered piece of the sentence was true.

Scattered pieces of Isaac said this phrase: "sensory seeking movement and behavior" again and again. I remember looking through that two-way mirror watching him stand on the chair then climb to the table and jump landing over and over again. I wanted to my mind to silence the rest of the scattered words. To get back to the river of denial, but it was no good.

Symbolically, the scattered pieces of the files on the floor had shared a deep truth that began to take shape as a puzzle does; one piece at a time. This puzzle had different shaped pieces and colors—nothing looked uninformed. There wasn't a picture on the cover of the "puzzle box." There wasn't a reference on how to even start to put this puzzle together.

When I looked at the scattered mess, I symbolically saw one fraction of a corner put together, a center spot, and one grouping off to the left and up just a bit. It was like I was surrounded by 500,000 more pieces and no guidance. I felt no hope, no light. Thad lived in his beautiful mind, and I lived in scattered, shattered pieces.

CHAPTER 17

# Margaret Susanna: My Pearl of Beauty

Scrape, scrape, scrape, and scrape the orange shell of the pumpkin clean from the pulp and seeds with my big metal spoon. With my sharp knife I sliced and cut out triangles, circles, squares, and jagged teeth; they all popped out of the hollow shells. Garrett looked at the creations and started to flap and jump around. Kellis wanted the candles lit and Isaac was swinging on the branch of the tree out front of the rental home. Tomorrow would be Halloween! I lifted the pumpkin up onto the porch bumping my belly in the process. I was as round as that pumpkin. *There*, I thought, *the fourth pumpkin finished.*

The morning of Halloween was a Friday morning and we were getting ready for trick or treating later that night. Around 11 in the morning I waved goodbye to the three boys as they sat on the porch with grandma placing the pumpkins in the order down the steps. I left for my doctor's appointment, my last before this baby would be born next week. My mind reflected on the past nine months and all that had transpired in my six years of marriage: 1) Finishing the build of our lives—The Red House, 2) the three moves from the basement to the trailer on the property, then to a rental in Ogden all because we were being followed and on the advice of John. 3) The shift in Thad's light back into shadow and addiction. All of the stress washed over me in waves and waves of darkness. Then I would fight to find light, but fear would return in mockery; then darkness again.

My reflection drove down deeper: I was a fool to trust Thad again and bring another life in to this mess. I was too forgiving and trusting. I would be having this little baby sometime next week, and I would be bringing him or her in to a world of chaos. I parked the car, opened the door to step out when a sudden pain shot down my back. My breath caught in my throat! The intensity ended as soon as it happened. I refused to believe what I knew to be true and walked up to the doors of the office tower, pushed my way inside, found the button on the elevator, and pressed up.

> *My reflection drove down deeper: I was a fool to trust Thad again and bring another life in to this mess.*

Again, the sharp pain shot down my leg I caught my breath again. I straightened back up doing a few deeps breaths, walked through the open doors of the elevator, and headed up to the office. It was time for my appointment and time to just rest. I checked in, found my comfy seat, and suddenly my name was called. I got up from the chair and for the third time, the lightning bolt of pain shot down my leg. I waddled through the door and just brushed off the pain. I was weighed; I peed in the cup and was shown to the room. I stripped my bottoms off used the tissue-thin exam blanket to cover me, and rested on the table until the doctor came in.

The doctor entered the room and asked how I was doing. I responded with fine and that I was looking forward to Halloween with my boys tonight. He checked things over and smiled. I did not return the smile. Right then for the fifth time the leg pain returned. He said, "You're going to miss trick or treating tonight." My head came up off the table. What? Was he serious? Not tonight—I wanted to be there for my boys! They needed to not miss this holiday and be disappointed again.

Nevertheless, it was true. I was in labor, and hot tears dripped off my face. It was the fastest emotion to pop up because a wave of stress came over me. I needed to make sure that the boys were NOT going to miss trick or treating. I wiped my face and I got dressed. I called home and told my mom that they needed to take the boys trick or treating because I was in labor headed to the delivery room. The shock was in my mom's voice and I asked her to reach dad and Thad. She promised she would, and I waddled down the hall from my doctor's office to the labor and delivery ward in the hospital.

Baby number four thought that this would be a great night to arrive. I remember passing the window before entering the hospital ward. When I had walked into the building it was in the 60's with a warm southern wind, but within 40 minutes the weather had turned. The winds shifted from the north. I watched the first flakes of snow starting to fall. Snow for Halloween? That was out of my hands, and I would just have to believe that the children would have Halloween.

As I checked in to labor and delivery, a sharp pain wrenched the side of my stomach. The pain had moved from my leg to my belly. The nurses helped me breathe through it and got me ready in a labor room. I laid there listening to the rapid heartbeat through the monitor of my unborn baby. Would this baby be a girl or a boy? I called Thad and left a message. He would either make it or not. I was alone for the first two hours of labor, which gave me time to reflect. I could feel the cycle of abuse starting once again although I never used the word abuse in referring to me. I only used it in referring to Thad and his demons.

I had overheard Thad on the phone with John two weeks ago, and he had started disappearing again. I knew the pattern. I knew the drill. I knew that I would be adding one more child to this craziness, but I knew the Heavenly Father was with me. I knew that I would be sustained. I knew that we would get support. Suddenly, a very sharp pain wrenched my back. I realized that I finally needed some support with this labor. I called the nurse telling them it was time for the relief from the pain. The clock ticked by in loud crashing clicks on the clock. I waited 40 minutes and finally, the team came in. I rounded my back as much as possible as I felt the long cold needle puncture my spine and the warm rush of fluid be released into my back.

As the medicine shot into my back, the foggy feeling and darkness started to creep into my body. Thad suddenly was there. He opened the door to the room and came to my side and held my hand. I smiled at him as I adjusted myself on the bed. But something was wrong. As I laid down, there was a warm rush of fluids from my back which seemed to be filling up my chest and my left leg. Suddenly I was very heavy; it was hard to think, I kept hearing the ding of a bell as I watched the snowfall. I could almost see each flake as it descended onto the windowsill of my hospital room.

A heavy feeling kept washing over me. I felt like I had peanut butter pumping through my veins, and it was getting harder and harder to breathe. I fought hard to sit up for breath, but the nurses turned me back to the bed to settle me in again. This was not right. Each time I tried to take a breath, it was like trying to breathe through a nearly blocked straw. My stats were dropping, and the nurse put oxygen on me to bring up the number.

Even with the help of the oxygen, I still couldn't settle into a breathing pattern. I remember thinking that everyone was getting quiet, that I couldn't hear them anymore. I kept telling the nurse that I was heavy and couldn't breathe but she kept looking at the IV bag. I could *not* understand. All my words were in slow motion. I felt an oxygen mask be placed over my mouth, but no matter what they did I was getting heavier and heavier. I kept watching the snow pile up on the windowsill. And my eyes got heavier and the feeling of sleep overcame me. My blood pressure was dropping, and the noise in the room became distant.

I was relaxing in to sleep. It felt warm, I felt lighter, and the room was getting brighter. I had a sense of home surrounding me and I wanted to stay where it was warm, bright, and like home. The feeling of home was like my grandma's at Christmas. I had a sense that my grandma was there with me in this peaceful light. The warmth and light seemed to consume me. I felt peace and never wanted to leave.

I remember *feeling* my grandmother near me. She gave me an impression, "if you stay here with me, you will find calm and peace, and if you return, you will have opportunities to grow and find what you are looking for." It was surreal. I had a choice. I felt love and peace and warmth with her. I was staying! Why would I leave? Then suddenly I felt a tug, a tug on my back, and I felt myself leaving. I remember feeling this understanding, "it was time to leave here and go back." I turned to where I felt my grandma, and I was filled with an impression. *I'm watching over you, we all are.*

Suddenly, I felt myself being tugged and pulled on me. I was leaving this warm place that felt like home with my grandma. I never really saw her, I only felt her. The feeling that I needed to do something started pulling me back to the delivery room. Soon the peace and warmth that I felt were replaced with the sound of a soft bell, like that of a jingle bell ringing. The ding of the bell was rhythmic, and it was calling me back. I needed to find my breath, but the pressure was building and building. The warmth and light were fading. Suddenly, I needed to push!

With that urge, I began to feel a pain in my chest, like a hammer there had hit me. My sternum was sore, and my left arm was being shaken and shaken by the nurse. The warmth of the serum ran in to my right arm and suddenly my heart felt like I was running a marathon. I was back. The dinging of the bells and alarms stopped and my breathing with the help of oxygen was better. I had nurses and doctors running from one side of the bed to the other side of the bed. "Welcome back, you're back!" She looked me dead in the eye, "no one leaves on my watch. We'll make it." I could only half smile. My chest felt lighter, but still, it felt like only one lung was working. It didn't matter, I was back and now I had to focus on the job I had to do the pressure was mounting.

The impression and words that my grandma left me with kept circulating in my mind over and over again. *I'm watching over you, we all are.* I wanted to feel her again, remember her again, and be with her again—the warmth that flooded my soul with love and peace was indescribable. Suddenly, stress and waves of emotions sent the final amount of pressure—it was time.

I looked at my doctor and got ready to push. Breathe, count, hold it, and push, push. My chest was on fire and the pain at my sternum killing me when I pushed. With shaking deep breaths, I breathed and pushed and pushed. The head was crowning. We were getting there. The nurse kept tapping me, "focus on the baby. Focus on now. Big, deep breath, and push!" I was delivering my baby and had a clear direction and purpose to what I was doing. I pushed, and pushed, and prayed for strength to endure through this delivery.

Soon relief replaced the building pressure; by joy and by the announcement that it was a girl! A girl had been born on this snowy Halloween night! They cleaned her up quickly and placed her on my chest. I remember holding her, hugging her, and praying to have the strength to find joy and endure. In that very vulnerable moment of life and death, life had won. As she whimpered and cried, I nestled her to me to nurse and thought *feed her; bring her your love.* I felt her latch on and a warm trickle began to flow from me to her. The light was being funneled through me to her. I clung to that light for I knew more darkness was coming. Thad turned to me and said, "John is back", and in that instant my wisp of light went out.

# CHAPTER 18

# *Mind Friends: They Comfort & Feed One yet, Starve the Other*

John was back. He kept telling Thad that he would have success with the Parade of Homes—that he would even win! Thad focused in on the work from January to June 2004. John never left his side. I would grit my teeth at the mention of John but for good or ill, John really had pulled him through it. Thad finished the house at the deadline. The two weeks of the Parade were amazing! The parade really pushed Thad and his Revolutionary Homes in to the limelight, and we won.

John kept talking about the power Thad had because of his success with the parade. Thad knew this was true because John believed every word of it. It was real to Thad. John told him of his influence, his fame, everything. His *mind*' and his drugs had such a power over Thad that they h over his rational thoughts and left paranoia in its w

Paranoia.

July 2004. Paranoia came just in time for our family vacation to my sister's home in Idaho. I had prepared everything I could think of to make the trip worthwhile. I thought that getting away and just enjoying being around family would be nice. We visited with cousins, connected with old friends in Idaho, and felt welcomed by so many. On the third night, however, a shadow crept in to our lives that would never leave.

I wanted to be with Thad, to keep my eye on him. He usually would have driven away for the "think time", but this night I stayed up late with him and we watched Jay Leno on the *Tonight Show*. I figured it would be fun and would be a great break—to laugh together.

During the opening monologue of the show, Jay Leno started talking about a general contractor he saw in McDonald's. He described the events and what happened with the general contractor and then made his joke. With that joke, Thad literally flew off the couch and turned off the TV. He started shouting at me, "Where are the cameras? Where are the cameras?!"

His eyes were frantic as he felt the walls of the home for a peephole—a camera. He ripped off family photos from the wall flinging them about the room until the walls were stripped bare. Beads of sweat quickly formed on his head and started running down his neck. He paced back and forth, "Where are the cameras??" I didn't know what he was talking about! All I could shout back was "What cameras?"

His eyes shifted from left to right, back to me, then left and right as his feet took slow steps back towards the wall. His eyes were wild, yet they were empty of light. His breath was like a dragon and with each sucking breath his paranoia was being fueled. He was in a state of mind that was not in reality. He turned to me with wild eyes raking over my face for a sign, a clue that I really knew where the hidden cameras were.

My face was pained and confused as I stared back. His dragon-type deep breaths began to slow his frantic pacing, then suddenly he turned, looked at the TV then twisted his head back to me and yelled, "I was that general contractor that Jay Leno was talking about during the monologue. Who knew that? I am on vacation and they are *still* following me. Why did you call them? How do you know them?"

My confused mind was racing for answers and nothing could escape my lips but truth and reason. "Jay Leno lives in California. They tape the show a day ahead of time. Thad, Jay was *never* talking about you!" Thad locked eyes with me and whisper-shouted, "How did he describe everything that I did today at McDonald's?" My voice caught—there was no answer to satisfy his paranoia. My mind was shouting, "What are you talking about?" repeated in my mind again and again, but nothing came out of my mouth.

With his eye locked on me, he lunged forward and grabbed the sides of my arms, and he lifted me off the couch and held me in the air.

The grip he had on my arms was shredding my skin as his fingers dug in to secure the hold he had on me. My breath caught while I was in the air! I dangled there in the air as his grip tightened around me. It happened so fast I didn't even cry out! He searched my face, raking

> *The grip he had on my arms was shredding my skin as his fingers dug in to secure the hold he had on me.*

over my eyes! Over and over he searched for a sign that I was lying. He kept gripping my arms firm by digging into my skin. He was waiting for me to tell him all about the cameras and anything else.

Then just as suddenly as his panic had started, it switched off! He released the grip on my arms and I dropped back to the couch in a heap. I took a deep breath and rubbed my arms. I could feel warm sticky fluid rushing to the area; blood.

My arms were bleeding. I grabbed my nursing blanket and applied some pressure until the bleeding stopped. Thad closed his eyes, shook his head and then opened them again. His face split in to that smile—that evil smile! Thad stopped his panic just as it had begun. My mind kept stammering over what he said, 'where are the cameras', but what my mouth asked was if he was ok.

He was silent—stone silent. Then his face changed. It was like a shadow crossed over, robbing his eyes of the last bit of light left. I rubbed my sore arms and watched him laid down and instantly started sleeping. I crawled to my diaper bag and applied Band-Aids to the backs of my arms. It was just scratched on the surface. But the bruising would come. How would I cover that? It was hot! It was summer. What could I do? I glanced back at Thad. His chest was rising and falling in a sleep pattern.

I collapsed on my sleeping bag in exhaustion with my head still spinning with what I had witnessed. Darkness, silence, racing thoughts, but the exhaustion and emotional fatigue seemed to creep up on me until it overcame my mind and hit the off switch. I was overcome with sleep.

Around three in the morning, Maggie-Sue woke up for her feeding and I looked over to a place where Thad should have been, but he was gone. An empty crumble of blankets told me he had left in a hurry, but that was the only clue I had. I nestled Maggie close to me and spent the rest of the night nursing her. I allowed my thoughts to spin and spin until the soft rosy color in the eastern sky told me that dawn would soon follow. It would be time to climb down the long steep flight of stairs and face the family, the breakfast, the day, with no answers as to where Thad was. I would come up with some type of story as usual.

When the questions came about to where Thad was, I told everyone that he was checking on a few job sites and would be back in time for the BBQ and for fireworks for tonight was the 4th of July. Their cousins distracted my children, but I was obsessing about the night's events. What did Thad mean that people saw him at "the" McDonalds? What was happening? Why had he physically grabbed me? Bruises were forming on the back of my arms under the Band-Aids. How was I going to hide that?

I half talked and half prayed throughout the day, searching for some kind of logic while trying to meet the needs of the children. No logic could be found to why he said what he did, and so I just went on with the day. Thad made it back for the fireworks, but he was altered. This was different than just being on drugs. He was not the same as just being on drugs or drunk, there was a difference in how he walked, acted, and even laughed.

His mindset, the split personalities, and amplified paranoia, this was all different. I never really saw Thad the same again for the next four years following the "Jay Leno" night. There were rare glimpses of Thad again, but just glimpses. The 4th of July the fireworks went off with flare and style. I watched my little ones jump and dance around. The fireworks and fun would only remember happiness associated with this 4th of July 2004 with cousins. However, when the last flash and pop of the fireworks went out, so did a little more of my hope and light.

The following day, I packed up everything by myself. The van was there for us, but Thad must have been walking for he was nowhere to be seen. I lifted it all to the car, alone, and then went inside and kept the conversation light with everyone. I hugged my sister and whispered my many thanks for hosting us and for making us feel so loved and welcomed. I clicked the buckle on the last of the four children and hopped in the van to go home. Thad was there just in time to climb in the van and drive away with us.

The only sound in the car was the whirl of the tires on the pavement. The children were asleep, and it was just Thad and me. We didn't talk, we didn't look at each other, and we just focused in on the road for the first hour. We simply let the turning tires propel us down the road back towards Utah and home.

After some time, Thad said one word, "freedom." I heard him say it and turned my head but did not verbally respond. More miles fell beneath us. He said it again, "freedom!" Then he began to talk. He told me about his life before we were married. He told me about his mind friends (he didn't call them that but that was whom he was referring to at the time), and what was happening to him now. Thad was very direct in telling me his paranoia and fear. He told me that people were watching him, watching all of us. He told me why people were watching him—because of his fame from the Red House and from the Parade of Homes. Once Thad started, he couldn't stop. He kept going on and on, story after story, example after example of how he was followed, monitored, and filmed at all times.

He explained that whenever he pulled in to gas stations or grocery stores that others who would also pull in were there because of him. They were watching and waiting for him. My shock and my disbelief were glaring from my face—WHAT?? That was NOT true! My body language and face told him about my disbelief. He smirked and smiled and shook his head as if to say, "you'll see." As the pavement went by, the stories rolled on and my mind was screaming that this was all crazy talk!!

Thad explained that at first, it was hard for him to get used to everyone following him. John told him to be strong and to just accept it. John? John! Thad said he took that advice and he accepted it. Thad then turned to me very seriously and said that it would be good for me to get used to being followed as well. That sentence did something to me, and I flipped out! I was now the one in a panic attack. I was breathing heavy and screaming at him to stop it—stop telling such lies!! That was not true!

I screamed at him, "John is NOT real! No one knows you for your business, for your ideas, for your family! No one knows us! No one follows us!" His eyes were dilated, and he just smiled and said, "watch." I told him he was delusional and that I didn't want to hear anymore unless he was willing to go and get help. I begged him to go and get help. I begged him! I begged him! He just smiled and said to watch for it to happen—that people were watching him and watching us as the miles rolled under the van.

Two years ago, we had watched the movie *A Beautiful Mind;* the conversation and the events that followed that were rare. Thad had seen that he had frightened me by his identifying with the main character. He had seen that he was going to have to keep his friends close to his heart and not reveal the truth of it. John advised him on that. John stated that he really needed to keep his cool in order for the business to be successful and for the Parade of Homes to really happen.

That event on our vacation was the beginning of my awareness of countless other *mind friend* delusional events. A day later he told me of the second event was that he claimed that Revolutionary Homes is so powerful that the United States Mint contacted him and asked him permission to use "We the People" on the $10 bill. He claimed that the phone call was untraceable because of the secret nature of national security. That was a lie. No one ever called and asked Thad for his permission, but he was convinced that it happened.

He rambled on to the third claim and that it was because of the 2004 Parade of Homes. He received a phone call from the Chevrolet Company—back in Detroit—asking him permission if they could use part of his company's name for a new campaign they were launching. The new Chevy Logo turned out to be, "Chevy, An American Revolution." I was shrieking with anger and yelling at him to STOP! I ran into his office and grabbed the stash of drugs that he had and flushed them all down the toilet. This was madness!

Thad's stories continued and his *mind friends* grew stronger and stronger until one day they seemed to split him in to two people. He started talking to himself more and more, pacing more and more and was so lost in his own thoughts. I wouldn't see Thad for hours or even days at a time. I felt so powerless, so hopeless. This spiral effect happened within the month of July 2004. I was so consumed with the need to have enough money for food and to pay the bills. Thad feed his mind friends and starved us. There was another factor on all of this; I was forced to learn how to work with autism and the intense sensory needs of the children, that I would just have to let Thad's *mind friends* go.

> *Thad's stories continued and his mind friends grew stronger and stronger until one day they seemed to split him in to two people.*

One day, Thad came home so excited and so filled with confidence and was pumping his fist over and over again in the air. Thad, with wild eyes and excitement, told me how he was Thomas Jefferson. He could feel the influence of Thomas! Then he turned his body away from mine and turned back and in that instance, his character, his manners changed. His voice changed, and Thomas Jefferson stood before me. Thad shouted that "he was powerful and influential!" Then he told me what happened that afternoon: Thad said he hired African Americans to drive his truck for him while he visited the different job sites. He sat in the back—in the bed of the truck—and shouted to the "Negroes" to DRIVE! DRIVE on—like slaves you were!!"

He turned to me and smiled like a madman! The scene was so surreal I felt like I was watching a movie. I was screaming in my head *what is happening??* But no words came out. I wanted to slap him, hit him, and have him wake up!!! But I was frozen where I stood. Thad told me where they drove him. He was shouting and pumping his fist! "I was in charge! I was the boss! I would never be captured again!" His eyes were wild and bloodshot. I am meant to be FREE!

Thad's shouting brought Garrett into the room. Garrett was so upset by the noise that he started screaming and crying. Garrett's screaming added panic to Thad's paranoia and he looked frantic. Then suddenly, Thad turned away from Garrett's screaming and ran towards the door. Just as he grasped the handle he turned and screamed with a full open spit flying scream of rage towards Garrett! "I WILL have my FREEDOM!" I turned my body to protect Garrett; He struck one blow across my back leaving me gasping for air, and that's when Thad RAN out of the house. I did not look up, and I did not look out the door until I no longer heard Thad's screaming. I was trembling with fear—shocked, shattered, and trying to figure out how to breathe.

Similar events happened several times throughout the summer of 2004. And I just would find a place of safety because I could not plan. I could not predict Thad's psychotic alterations/episodes. All I could do was hope to make it another day.

I knew that Thad needed help. I begged, I pleaded; I even drove him to the hospital one night when he was in this state of mind, but because Thad was an adult and told the doctors that he didn't want treatment, there was nothing to do unless he actually physically assaulted someone or chose to get help for his mental illness. I was drowning, choking, within this non-reality world and the reality of caring for the family.

I was going to be alone forever raising the children while Thad listened to his *mind friends*, did drugs, starved us by his neglect, and gave away the money to John. I would just stare at him and more and more stories spewed from his mouth. I had no response. I had to run in to my world of helping the kids. My sons' autism was better than this world of Thad.

The journey in to this madness of his mind was not beautiful. It was warped and twisted. It was bleak and dark. It was one more thing to worry about besides getting help for my children. Thad just became someone else to worry about, pray for, and to fight with. I did not have a marriage. I was someone who cleaned the big Red House to show off as a model home, I took care of four children under the age of six, I did therapy with three of them with autism, and to tried to feed the family for less than $200 a month for food. I was a slave to our creation, and Thad was in the office creating more of a darker and darker prison for us all.

Why did I stay? I was trapped. No money, no ability to financially care for my children, and what do you say to others? Did I marry someone based on hope? I rolled the dice on the risk of his history (that I knew of with the addiction) but not his mental illness. The abuse seemed to just roll with the illness. It was something that made a combination that I was now familiar with, but I could not predict.

I've heard about abuse and the different types of people who abuse and why they do. I was again denying that I was abused. In order to understand it, I put it into two categories. The Hunter and the Caged Animal: 1) the hunter has control, 2) has a plan, and 3) acts out the plans with the intent to hurt, damage and control. The caged animal: 1) has intense paranoia, 2) feels no control of life, 3) acts out of fear, and 4) is not in control of their rage. I was definitely *not* married to a hunter. I was facing a caged animal that wanted their freedom. Is one more dangerous than the other? Time would only tell.

# SECTION 5

# Near Kills: When you are distracted, you take your eye off the enemy

# CHAPTER 19

# Wooden Prison: Dreams Turn to Nightmares

Ting, ting...ting, came the sound in to the warm night air. The noise came from the sound of Thad's gold wedding ring as he chucked it down the street. The next sound was that of a slamming truck door, the starting of the engine, and the squealing of tires on loose gravel as Thad sped away from me. My teeth were clenched tight, my daughter was wrapped tightly around my neck and waist, and my hot eyes were focused on the reflection of the glint of gold, as it lay among the construction heap in the far corner of the property. I stomped over to the pile and picked up the ring. If that was how he felt about everything, then I would sell the ring for cash.

The money from the ring gave us some groceries and a small Christmas. Christmas faded to New Year's and I sighed as I put away the last Christmas ornament and put the lid on the box. It was January 2005. I lifted the box onto the shelf and caught my breath, a wave of nausea washed over me. I stood there holding the shelf in panic. I was going to be sick. I knew this sickness and it was going to last for another seven months. I gripped that shelf so tight I wanted to break it off. I had only given in to Thad's needs once. It had been months and months! This was not possible! How was I going to do this??

I turned from the shelves and as I climbed up each step from the basement, it was like a weight was added to me. Another baby. Step. Four other children to care for. Step. Three of my children have autism. Step. One has severe developmental and language delays. Step. Grinding debt. Step. Thad's double life and mental illness. Step. No real friends. Step. No source of income. Step. I was in survival mode. Step. I had no hope left. Step.

I walked into the family room and I stoked up the fire with more wood from the construction bin before setting the grate in front of the fire. I watched the flames lick and tease the icy frozen wood as a child licks a Popsicle in summer. The sizzle and pop of the ice and water as the heat reached it gave me some hope that we might warm my room above it. The propane was nearly gone. I ran the heat for 1 hour in the morning and for one hour in the evening and then shut it off. That way it was around 55 in the house. The pipes would hold and not freeze tonight.

I turned from the fire and climbed up the stairs to the second level. There at the top of the stairs, I watched each one of my children's chests rise and fall in a rhythmic pattern under their layers of quilts. Their gentle breaths escaped their open mouths. My thoughts were for them to dream; to dream for better, for more, for peace, and it may come to them. As my hand released the knob from the last door I walked down the hall to the cold Master Bedroom. I remember thinking about nothing yet being overwhelmed by everything. I couldn't sleep, so I just sat in bed and felt empty.

Suddenly, I was shaken from the place in between sleep and thoughts by a phone call. I looked at the clock. 2:30 am. I answered. Hello? A sharp voice on the other end of the line, "Will you accepted the charges of a collect call?" "What?" was my response? "Will you accept the charges of a collect call?" "Yes," came my weak replay. It was Thad. He was in jail. He had been arrested for a DUI and possession of drugs.

Thad sounded so empty and so hollow. He begged me to get a hold of John. That John would fix it. John would bail him out. It felt surreal...like I was in a movie and at any moment someone was going to yell "cut..." and it would all be over. "John??" I shouted! "He won't come for you tonight!" Suddenly the phone call was disconnected. I held the phone in my shaking hand and hung up. Almost out of habit or even a reflex, I called my father-in-law and relayed the story.

Following that phone call to him, I just sat there in the cold dark. I didn't sleep. I just waited for the blackness of the night to lift and for the day to start. That was a dark black night. I knew that if I stayed in the relationship, or stayed physically in the Red House, the darkness would never leave. I would be lost in this world of madness forever. I knew I must leave—at least for a while. This was my chance to do so, therefore I aimed myself towards the small fraction of light I could see and pressed on through the darkening night of my life.

## CHAPTER 20

# Basements: Beginning, Middle, and Ending

I have many "basements" of my life. Our marriage started in a basement and ended in one. It was almost prophetic. The days spent beneath the earth with little sunshine to illuminate our lives…the long nights of sleeplessness…the cold creeping in and grasping at your feet and allowing it to wrap around your body while struggling to keep warm, keep happy, and to survive. The basement became a place where our marriage began and where it, eventually, ended.

We moved in and out of basements depending on what our choices in our marriage had been: built a new home, moving to a new home, move out of the basement. Not have enough work, sell the home, and move back to the basement. Find work, build another spec home, move out of the basement. Sell the spec home, moving back into the basement. Do you see the pattern? Three basements each have names and stories:

Layton basement, Red House basement, and Yellow House basement.

Layton Basement: The Layton basement held for us our first home and a place to be proud of. We had taken an old musty dirt basement and had remodeled it and transformed it in to a home. We had a large Master Bedroom, a wonderful jetted tub, a functional kitchen, a large living room, mudroom, washroom, and a place to entertain. It was the beginning of our marriage and then it was time to leave the basement in June 1998.

We moved back to the Layton basement in December 2001. We moved back following the time we lived in Idaho. To come back to that basement was an embarrassment. It was dark, and I was filled with shame and pain, but felt I had no choice but to make the marriage work. We moved back to the basement in order to survive. We moved back because there was nothing left for us in Idaho. We were refugees from our own battles: Thad's adultery, and my fighting to desperately hold to our marriage that was slipping through my hands like smoke. But now, the basement had to hold a place for three children—three beautiful, young, pained, and innocent children. It was a mark of failure for me, but a place of refuge for the children.

The Red House basement: this was a place where I created a business from and allowed for some cash/money to flow. I taught tumbling and cheerleading in the basement. I also ran a preschool for a few months there. I tried to keep up the positive attitude to stave off the madness that was our life. The Red House was definitely filled with our sacrifice almost like blood. But it too was dark, cold, and lonely.

The Yellow House basement: this place was in Huntsville in my parent's home. This basement became a place of refuge for me, once I had separated from Thad and the Red House. I needed a place to stay. I was carrying our fifth child (my baby had been conceived in another lie). I had Thad frame up the walls, and then ask him to leave. My father and I worked on coordinating the electrical, plumbing, heating insulation, and sheet rocking, and then I would lay the flooring, do the painting, and hang the cabinets. I just needed Thad to put up the walls, and then I took those walls and turned them in to my family's fort to fight off the madness, try to enclose happiness, and heal.

The Yellow House basement had its sharp and stinging moments too. I was laying the laminate flooring by myself, and I had asked for some neighbors to help me. All the neighbors knew what Thad's habits were. Many of them knew before I did that Thad had fallen "off the wagon again," and those neighbors would never talk to me about it. They talked about it with each other but not to me, until the time I was laying the laminate flooring in the Yellow House basement.

One of my neighbors, (I'll call him David) came to help me with the flooring, and he also had quite a mouthful to tell me. I remember bending over the laminate flooring, trying to fit it, cut it, slide it with my round belly in the way, and my neighbor just lit in to me.

David was a father of three children at the time, and he was there to represent the neighborhood. He told me that all six families (who lived in the neighborhood) knew about Thad and the drugs and drinking. They all wanted to say something to me to help but didn't dare or know how, so David was nominated to help me to see the reality of my life. The conversation of "what are you going to do?" was repeated over and over at me. He was asking and asking if I was going to finally divorce Thad! He was asking if I was going to finally break the abuse cycle and get the kids in to a healthier place.

I had literally had worked the laminate flooring in to a corner, and I had no escape from his truthful stinging words. David saw it as he "was just trying to help my family." He kept asking with shouting tones, "How are you going to raise them (the kids)? How are you going to feed them? How are you going to protect them?" I could feel his rising anger with each word because his childhood came from a very similar place.

He looked at me with disgust and with pity. He firmly spoke these words and stared at my bulging pregnant tummy. His eyes flashed from there to my face catching my eyes, my watering burning eyes. "April, what are you going to do? How are you going to feed your kids? They can't eat off the nothingness anymore. You are the only one that can help them; you need to do something. You need a plan. You've got to get it together or otherwise your boys will follow Thad in to his habits. They will. You mark my words...they will follow the same hell that has been laid out for you unless you break the cycle and leave Thad."

My stomach was lurching, my eyes were swelling from the hot angry tears, and I had no place to run to. I was cornered. He knew he had said too much and he just left slamming the door out of frustration and embarrassment. I collapsed to the floor and felt so destroyed. My spirit could not handle the depth of pain and shame that I felt.

From where I sat, my eye caught my image reflecting back to me from the bathroom mirror. I looked at my pathetic scene: purple bags under my eyes, my hair greasy and matted from working, and I was pregnant with my fifth child. The list continued: no home to live in, separated from a husband, no value, and no self-worth.

I just rubbed my belly and rubbed my head. I remember calling on my Heavenly Father to send me support. I had to finish the floor that day because the carpet was to be laid the next day. I could only focus minute to minute. I was in no shape to think about the future, just lay and snap in the next piece of flooring before the children return from school and before Margaret woke up and needed feeding. I dried my eyes and started to hammer, snap, hammer, and snap...

The Yellow House basement was also my place of refuge. It was filled with people who loved me throughout the construction. Friends and church members, mothers and fathers, and dear loving people came to help with cabinets, painting, and ultimately moving in the furniture. They shared hugs of support with me. They shared powerful strength giving speeches with me. I felt their love and it helped me to find the energy to finish it. I had organized it, completed it, and now I was going to recover from it. I needed to have a place to fill the love of the Lord, look at the sunrise, and know that we were going to make it.

My place of refuge was finished; it was complete. I was now going to live in my parent's newly remodeled basement and think, pray, and figure out a plan for my children's lives and mine. I had to have geographical distance from Thad in order to use logic and not emotion. Logic led me to a simple statement of divorce, emotion led me in to dark cloud smothering choking thoughts.

I would change my mind based on emotions. My mind would have great shifts. I will divorce him. I won't divorce him. I will just teach him a lesson. I will just hold onto a thought, or a fairy tale, or a dream, or is it a dream that will just turn to smoke? I kicked him out in February 2005, lived in a world of separation which was neither final or on. It was just an "in-between world." I was hormonal and weak from the pregnancy. I was spiteful and pathetic. My mind would hold firm to the separation working on a divorce, but my heart would collapse with thoughts of I would bring shame to the family; "the one who was divorced." The irony of that statement was that my family was saying the opposite: get out and be free!

I was free from Thad's madness and mind while I stayed in the Yellow House basement, but I was very overwhelmed with three children with autism, and one little girl with severe learning, language, and gross motor delays. I was trying to help them, think about them, feed them, teach them, and yet keep my body fighting to live another day of the uncertainty to nurture another life.

During Margaret's nap time, I would sit for hours on the computer looking at ways to get a divorce and the deep costs associated with it: both financially, and spiritually. But the divorce debate always came down to custody. I never knew when he was sober, high, drunk, talking to his other self or a combination. What would he be like when the children went over there? The children were in harm's way because of his bipolar impulses, split realities, and ultimately, his abuse. If I was divorced and was not able to get full custody, then I would lose my children to madness.

Finally, in June 2005, the pain in my womb started, and it marked the end of this nine-month journey which was founded on another set of lies, from the Red House, to building the Yellow House basement, to now delivery my fifth and final child of this unstable relationship.

I asked Thad to come to the hospital. In my second round of weakness, I had asked him back; it was my fleeting hope that through this birth we would heal, he would give up his druggy friends, and that we together and would make an honest return to faith…the family needed to be whole. Throughout the delivery he was there, well at least he was physically there.

I put up with the pain until it was time for the epidural. I remember thinking as the long sharp needle punctured my back that if Thad could see me near death, he might have an experience that would shake him back to the time of when he saved me from hitting my head in the shower. Maybe he could be shaken from his drugs and see me as he had done seven years ago. Maybe he would see me and want to save me like the time I fell in the shower and he caught me—he saved me! Do you see the audacity of that kind of hope?

The same peanut butter fog washed over me, but this time the nurses were ready. I fell in to the trance-like state right after I receive the epidural. It was at this place that I did not want to be alone; to bear a child alone without anyone there, I thought I would not make it.

Thad was physically there but emotionally numb. I was in transition and I did get very weak. I became very heavy with blackness and the room slowed down, the actions of the nurses slowed to half the regular pace, the voices became slurred, and the light in the corner of the room seemed to grow brighter. I remember reaching out for Thad's hand, touching it, holding it, but it was cold and clammy, it held no warmth in it. His hand was there, but his emotional connection towards us was not. I felt cheated, I felt cold, and the light in the corner was getting brighter. If I just walked to that light, then my darkness would be done.

Suddenly, I was shaken back by the nurse with short hair. She was looking at me, saying my name, telling me to focus, telling me to focus—to focus on her. Gently a trickle of warmth within my chest started to surge throughout my blood sending with its energy and consciousness. I looked at her and focused on her face, her encouragement, and her voice. I was back, and Thad was gone. The light had dimmed, and the pressure of my baby was back. I knew I had to look to the nurse and push, push, push.

With each push, I knew that I was going to have a beautiful little girl soon lifted into my arms. I knew I was going to have someone else to love and for them to love me back.

Finally, with the last push, she was here. She was blue, she didn't cry. I couldn't hear her cry! She was too quiet! She was quickly flashed before my eyes and then quickly taken to the warming table for a good rub down and more suctioning. She was too quiet! I looked at the table and lights and my baby. I was praying for my baby to breathe—to scream! Scream!! Finally, a weak little cry emerged from the bed. Her whiteness and blueness became pink and flushed. She began to breathe on her own and with her own strength. Soon she was wrapped tight and laid in my arms; my little Virginia Grace.

In my foolishness and weakness, I had decided to give Thad one last year. I was completing the cycle of insanity of doing the same thing over and over again in hoping that a different result would happen. Thad's habits never changed. I spent six nights a week alone, then I would lie to cover up Thad's drunkenness, and his mind friends to my parents. The year in the Yellow House basement was the same financially as if we lived in the Red House. I was lying to my parents again, but this time it was worse because we were living in their basement. I was getting sucked back in to old habits. The dark numbness and routine had returned. We were going nowhere drifting on a life raft with no direction.

Then suddenly—as if a sail had been attached to the life-boat—I was given an opportunity that would change my future life. I was asked to be a founding parent of Spectrum Academy. The year was dark, yet there was a ray of light and of hope of being a founding parent. Spectrum Academy would save my life in ways I could

*Then suddenly—as if a sail had been attached to the lifeboat—I was given an opportunity that would change my future life. I was asked to be a founding parent of Spectrum Academy.*

never imagine with all the chaos going on. It was the crucial part of living here in the Yellow House Basement with my parents. I had nagging words echoing in my head that I needed to break the cycle of abuse, of neglect, and to find a way to make our lives different. I was going to somehow. I was someday going to need to become the breadwinner.

There was also something to physically to plan on: it was the handcart trip to Wyoming. That was my focus and my goal to reach. I knew that it would set a pivot point for me. The story, the powerful memory of my ancestors crossing the plains unprepared or unaware of the physical danger they were stepping in to must be the last hope for us. My hope was that this journey on visiting Martin's Cove on the plains of Wyoming would strengthen our family to give us "one last chance." It did, but in a way that was not expected.

Basements. I've talked about The Layton basement, the Red House basement, the Yellow House basement, and once again, in a few weeks time, we would return to the Layton basement. It was the summer of 2006. Following our trip to Wyoming, we moved to that basement for the last time. It was fitting that our marriage started and ended in a dark basement. What was even more fitting, was the fact that it had started and would eventually end in the same dark Layton Basement.

# CHAPTER 21

# The Trip: Winds of Wyoming Cleared the Fog of my Life

Trip: a short getaway, a vacation, time physically away from home, to leave and then return later. Trips can be short or long. Sometimes they range from weeks in length to a few hours getaway. Planning occurs for all trips in order for them to have some sort of success. There was a start and a return date, items/food you will need on your trip, and travel plans on how you will get there and how you will return. For me, *The Trip* to Martin's Cove in Wyoming was going to only be four days total in length, however, the planning for this trip took nine months.

Martin's Cove was a small sheltered pocket on the south side of the Sweetwater Mountains where the Martin Company of handcart pioneers tried to take refuge from the raging

October blizzards in 1856. Over one-fourth of the 576 members of the company passed away in Wyoming.

I had ancestors who made their journey to Utah in this Company: the Parkinson family. Ellen Parkinson was five years old (the sixth of nine living children of John and Ellen Smalley Parkinson) when she traveled with her family in the Martin Handcart Company. John (father), Ellen (mother), and four of their nine children passed away on the trail in 1856. However, Ellen, only five years old, survived the frozen, bitter, Wyoming weather and made it to the Salt Lake Valley.

That story has always fascinated me; how the faith and strength of a five-year-old carried her through the toughest times. I had a connection with Ellen and over these past nine years of marriage, I began to really study her journey, her story after she arrived at the valley, the family who helped to raise her, and her married life. I drew more and more strength from her story; that she could do hard things and so could I.

I laid the last of the camping gear on the dining room table. There! The gear was all there. I looked over the packs. I smiled. After nine months of planning and gathering, we were ready. I opened the bedroom door and checked on the sleeping children one more time. Their soft lips and rhythmic breathing told me there were sleeping. With a skip in my step, I walked back to my bedroom and crawled in to bed. I looked over at Thad who was sitting in the chair and said, "We are ready!" His eyes smiled at me then spun upward and were locked towards the ceiling. He didn't move, but I saw his lips start in that familiar pattern of speaking without words. No! I screamed in my head. Not tonight! No mind friends tonight, I screamed in my head.

Thad then tipped his head down from the ceiling to me with dim eyes and said, "I'm not going. John needs me to stay here." My face felt the sting of Thad's words. He rose from the chair, and in a mechanical rhythm walked out of the bedroom and out the door. My heart was thumping and thumping faster and faster against my chest. The heat and hot flash of anger suddenly rose up. I grabbed a pillow and screamed that hot anger in to it again and again. I bit in to the soft fabric with rage and my grip became knuckle white on it.

I saw flashes of the past nine months (the meetings, the planning, the conversations) like a beam of light to hold on to as the darkness of life swirled around me, snuffed out! I marched around the room screaming and screaming in to the pillow. The searing hot tears fell into the fabric of the pillow leaving black mascara stains behind. My anger was at myself for allowing me hope! But, true to form, he quit! It was like the ray of light punching through the darkness had been sealed shut and I was left in the echo of the darkness.

As soon as I felt that darkness had crept in my heart, my feet stopped pounding and I collapsed onto the bed. Something snapped in my mind! It was a still small thought. *He said, "I'm not going." He never said WE are not going.* The thought was so powerful it was resonating like the sound waves of a tuning fork. WE—the children and me! We could go! We could do this. Another thought penetrated my soul. *You are the caregiver for the family. Now, go and bring them in to the light.*

I bolted up off my bed again and stood on my own two feet. As I stood there in the dark bedroom, I made a choice. I was not going to sit in the dark on this one. I was going to *feel* my way around the darkness of Thad's decision to not go with us until I found that trap door, ripped it open, spilling the light back onto our family.

As I stood in the bedroom in the Yellow House basement a final thought hit me: *Victim or Victor?* I stood on my feet looking across my empty bed. I looked at the empty room. I flicked on the lamp, and I looked over at the nightstand and found my book. I grabbed my book on the side of my bed that had Ellen's story in it and flipped through the pages until I came to the few recorded words again from her journal, she "was not going to freeze to death!" For her, that was not the option! I read that over and over again.

I needed to gain this strength from my fourth great-grandmother, and I needed to take my family on this trip. I was going to be a Victor, not a Victim. I could do it with the strength of the Lord and with the memory of Ellen with me. *I* needed this trip! *I* needed it for my sanity! I put the book back on the nightstand, flicked off the light, and got in to bed. VICTOR! I was shouting in my head! When morning came, I got all the kids up, and we left for Wyoming without him—Victor!

With each step I took in the sunbaked dirt and sagebrush, I could feel my ancestors with me. I could feel a sense of what drove them on—Faith in the Lord Jesus Christ. One challenging hike that proved this was called the "women's pull". All the men in the company were asked to stand on top of the ridge, and all the women pushed and pulled the carts up the hill without them. The women gathered strength and helped each other over and over as we went up the sandy hill. The men began to sing and clap and shout encouragement, and there was a power in that cheering. Through their cheering and singing from the men, there was a wave of strength that helped to push my cart up the hill—victory!

After a long night of a tent filled with autism challenges, the following day we forged the Sweetwater River in our handcarts. The crossing of the Sweetwater in the heat of June was NOTHING like it was in the fall of 1856. Ellen's descent into the river that fall had been filled with floating ice, trail-worn shoes, rags wrapped around hands and necks trying to stave off the bitter cold. Many of the company passed away due to the complications of forging the river in such conditions. There is a section of the river that is known as veil crossing—many following that crossing passed onto the next life.

When I stepped into the cool water in the searing heat of June, I felt refreshed, not destroyed. Following the first few steps into the river, I found myself pulling my cart and slipping on the rocks on the bottom on the riverbed and the current began sucking away my handcart from me, pulling my children away from my control. My seven-year-old tried to push from behind but soon found his feet being lifted off the bottom of the river. I could feel his body slip off the back of the cart and the current pick him up and all he could do was float. My children in the cart started to scream as the current carried us sideways pulling us downstream.

The current was still swift as I tried to find my footing. Our screams and cries for help were heard, and teams of people came to help me, and my children, find stable footing and get to the other side of the river. I had to rely on the help of others to bring my family to safety. This event was powerfully symbolic of what I was going to be experiencing five months later in my life.

After the Sweetwater crossing, I had another long night alone with my fitful children in the wilderness. The following morning it was time break down the camp, eat, pack the handcart and hike into Martin's Cove. Prior to entering in the cove, I parked my handcart alongside the rest of our company, watching the crossbar tip down like a seesaw allowing for a shady spot underneath. I quietly tucked my four-year-old in that shade to rest with other children who were exhausted. A sweet sister from my ward told me to go on ahead. She would stay with him. I thanked her and turned and faced the cove.

The Cove is a bend/pocket of the mountains where Ellen, as a five-year-old (with only three other siblings left alive from the family of 11 that started the journey), found safety. It was hallowed and sacred ground. With each step in to this hallowed ground, my mind's eye conjured up the frozen scene as circular mounds of stiff canvas lay on the ice and snow with faithful heartbeats from men, women, and children laid underneath them. Their emaciated bodies could no longer set up the tents so many just crawled underneath as the sub-zero temperatures gripped them. For some, the lumpy canvas would be their final earthly sleep never to wake again.

My fourth great-grandmother laid down in this cove in the ice and snows under a stiff canvas next to her mother, her sister, and her two brothers, only to wake the next morning to her mother's frozen body. She and her three siblings were left of the 11 who started out. My mind's eye turned off the icy scene and I looked at the aspens shimmering with their leaves and the soft grass of the cove. I thought, *the bleakness of winter rested her dark frozen hand here, wiping away the comfort of warmth and light from their worn bodies.* It was a powerful thought and held me there in the Cove for some time.

I knew the bleakness of my life felt like that journey for Ellen. Yet the past four days had pushed me to do things on my own. It had awakened something within me. The darkness of the abyss of abuse had closed off so much hope for me over the past nine years of marriage. Suddenly, I was comparing the heat and light of the cove on that day to my darkest days of the abyss of abuse. Something shifted inside me in the cove and I felt this prompting. *You will have a decision to make, the hardest of your life, soon. Remember the light of this moment and draw upon this for your darkest hour is yet to come.* I was rooted to the spot. The clarity of the feelings from those thoughts ran through me and seared in to my heart.

As my feet carried me out of the cove, I found myself gently lifting my family back in the cart. It was time to leave.

As I reached down to the crossbar and picked up my handcart again, I started the return trip to the campsite that was four miles away. With each step on the dusty road, I felt myself reflect upon the journey of pulling my family by myself yet, not alone. I had experienced having friends and neighbors to help me bear my journey and strengthen me when I needed it. I felt the Lord strengthen me by directing me and prompting me. I was strengthened; I could tackle the next bit of my life by myself with the Lord. With each step, I was setting new goals. I could see myself walking away from a dark storm and into the light again. I felt inspired! I felt encouragement! I felt that anything was possible, and I felt the power!

> *I could see myself walking away from a dark storm and into the light again. I felt inspired! I felt encouragement! I felt that anything was possible, and I felt the power!*

Then suddenly, like a sharpened ax slicing through wood, my hope, my power, and my strength were severed. It was Thad! I don't know how he got there or where he came from, but suddenly Thad was physically there and was right beside me near the handcart in Wyoming! He slipped in under the handle of the pull bar and wanted to join me in pulling the children. I was in shock! I actually gasped, dropped the bar, and jumped over the handle. My releasing the grip on the bar was so sudden that Thad was not ready for it, and the children slammed to the ground and were jolted around inside of the cart.

I found myself running and running into the open field. I ran into the field shouting and screaming. I ran and ran and ran! Thad? Here? How? I ran more. Here?? Now?? I screamed and shouted and shook my fists. This was not fair—Thad? He had left me at the last minute to pull my children in the hot sun, camp and cook with them, handle the autism outbursts in the wilderness without his support, putting on the moleskin on the blisters, treating the heat stroke, and then at the end of all my struggles he just showed up? He felt that he could just be a part of all my hard work, my blood sweat and tears? How dare he swoop in when the journey is finished to take the credit! I continued to scream out in the field. I knew I was making a show, but the emotion of that moment was overwhelming. I screamed and screamed towards the heavens until I collapsed on the hot dusty ground exhausted.

In that moment of exhaustion, I suddenly turned back to see my children crying and reaching out to me. I was in huge conflict! Everyone on the trail was watching this scene unfold. Our cart had blocked the path and held the ward in a gridlock pattern. They were watching me come apart in an open field, watching my children cry and reach out for me, and watching Thad stand there looking in the opposite direction. The kids! Their tears, their need for me drove me back to my feet. I swallowed my pride and marched through the field and to the back of the cart only for my children. I began pushing from the back of the cart as he pulled in the front. That was all I could do. The company then resumed their progress to the campsite and we finished our trek, the final two miles in silence.

With each heavy step I took, it stirred up more dust and had my head down to breathe in the choking clouds. I felt so conflicted, so torn. Nine months ago, during the planning stages, all I wanted was for us to go on this journey together, as a family. I wanted to find our way together in the wilderness, to feel the influence of my ancestors trying to help and uplift us from the dark choices that had overtaken our lives. I wanted to find the light again—with Thad. But his decision to back out at the last minute and dump us on our journey had left me with a pivot point.

Was I going to be victim or victor? I had fallen for the victim so many times I wanted to VOMIT! I wanted to be the victor! I wanted to prove that I could do this; that I can support my family, and that I no longer have to wait for Thad. No! His decision to leave at the last minute was not going to mend. This was the final wedge that placed me in a dark place of hurt and seething anger! How dare he just think that I can do all the work and then he gets to come in at the end and be the saint? No, this was a pivotal point—Victim or Victor?

During those last two dusty miles, I became Victor! I determined to take control of my life and to no longer be at the mercy of Thad's dark decisions. I was worthy of care. I was worthy of light. I was worthy of love. With each step of my grandmother's journey, I knew that I was going to have to become the breadwinner. I knew that I was going to have to create my own stability. I knew that Thad's mental health would have him in and out of our lives. I was no longer going to be a victim to him anymore. I was going to not wait for him to get it together in order to provide for us; I was going to find light and find a way to provide, somehow.

# CHAPTER 22

# *Spectrum: Building my Escape Route*

In general terms, *spectrum* means to classify something between two extreme/opposite points. It is a way to gain perspective through that measurement because you have a scale of one extreme to the other. Therefore, many things can have a spectrum attached to it, for instance, politics and light. Whenever the word spectrum was mentioned for me, it meant autism and the extreme opposite points that I lived with on a daily basis. However, the word spectrum soon meant to me stability, employment, and my freedom.

The word autism had been officially connected to my children ever since late 2002. When all three of my boys were diagnosed, they were identified on different points along the autism spectrum. I had a spectrum within my own home from verbal to nonverbal to extreme sensory needs to under sensitized sensory needs. It was incredibly challenging to raise my sons with stability and predictability because of the chaos we faced. The biggest challenge was trying to find stability and consistency and light when Thad was constantly bringing in darkness and chaos.

However, In the Yellow House Basement in December of 2005, one phone call was about to change my life and set us towards a course of freedom from the chaos. I was invited to become a founding parent of a charter school that would emphasize educating children who are on the autism spectrum. We were a group of eight parents with a variety of backgrounds, but we all had one thing in common: we all had someone in our family with autism.

When I said yes to be a founding parent and then a board member, there became some motivation and some hope for the education of my children for the fall of 2006. I knew that this would bring change to our family just in the fact that we would be adding a two-hour commute to try to get to school and back every day. However, there was a motivation for someone else; for me. I felt that this might be an opportunity for more than giving my children the education that they needed.

As founding parents, we all had a motivation to create a school that would fit their needs. Each parent had a committee they oversaw. I was over the enrollment. My job was to contact families by phone; processing the physical paperwork by typing it in to the database. Once the information was in the database, I had to maintain the database and verify requirements. I also had to follow up with the parents who submitted the applications and the accompanying documentation. I had to attend meetings two times a month and I did all of this in the chaos that we lived in.

There were dark months of 2005-2006 that I didn't know if I would have enough gas to drive to the meeting or if I could find a babysitter just so that I could attend the meeting. I tried to involve Thad in the excitement of building a school. Building a place for our children to be educated but he was not excited, not involved, and therefore not invested. However, it became my motivation to try to attend each meeting, find childcare, complete my enrollment assignments, contact the parents, and sell this school to everyone who I knew needed it. From the fall of 2005 to the summer of 2006 the Spectrum Academy was a huge part of my life, but little did I know how invested I would become until later that year.

Forward to July 2006: We had one month before the construction of the school would be finished and classes would start. Since I was so involved with enrollment, I did not know how the academic assignments and hiring processes were going. The news at this meeting was encouraging. They had filled each teaching position but one, and they had nearly all the curriculum. The construction of the build was set back by some late summer rains, but the construction company felt encouraged that they would be able to make up the time and get back on track. Soon, the meeting was wrapping up and I would be on my way back home.

Following this meeting, the board president approached me and asked me a question that would change the course of my life. She was very direct in asking me. She asked if I would be the fifth-grade teacher for Spectrum that fall of 2006. I was caught off guard. The visible look of shock was all over my face—complete with my opened mouth. She proceeded to give me a description of what it would entail, the curriculum, and the start date. Her final question to me was, would I accept the teaching position?

I remember thinking so many thoughts to myself: You have your bachelor's degree, but not a teaching license. You are great with kids in a gym setting, but what about a classroom? How would you teach and still be a mom? Would you have to move to Layton——to the basement again? You would need to be closer to the school. *You* would need to find childcare for the girls. But, *YOU* would have an income. *YOU* would have control. And, *YOU* would be the *light* for your family. All those thoughts poured over my head and heart. My mind flashed back to just a few days before when I was in the cove, *"you will have a decision to make, the hardest of your life, soon."* It was such a surreal experience; I found myself stammering out the word *YES!* I hugged her, and suddenly an avalanche of thoughts and feelings tumbled down on me! As turned to leave, I caught her eye one more time; I was REALLY going to provide for my family!

On my drive home, I began to think, and even dream! I would have a stable income. I would be able to provide for my children. Thad would continue to do or not do based on his mental stability, and for the first time, financially it wouldn't affect us! I would have three of my five children there with me at the school. I would need to find childcare for my two girls, but I had a feeling that it would all work out.

I had my bachelor's degree since 1998; I just needed to find a way to obtain my teaching certification while teaching. As I drove towards the Yellow House Basement, I found myself praying, and thanking God. I had tears of gratitude and a bursting heart of love. This was the answer. This was going to be the stability I had longed for nearly nine years. This was light! I suddenly felt overwhelmed with love because of the strength of my family, my ancestors, and my Heavenly Father. This was the answer.

Within one week, I had enrolled in a Master's of Special Education program, which also offered a teaching certification and licensure program. I also had been blessed to find a scholarship program that would pay for my degree as long as I taught in the state for four consecutive years. I opened my own bank account and I would hide the money there.

Everything was lining up! It was my Heavenly Father's light that sliced through the darkness once again for me.

From July 8th to the 21st, I repainted the Layton Basement, I laid laminate flooring, I figured out living space for all seven of us in a two-bedroom basement, I packed a house, I found the teaching program, I even had been given help to move the family for free, and I opened a separate bank account. By the end of July 31st, I moved the family from the Yellow House basement back to the Layton basement. This was the blessing that I had felt was going to come and it came with a gentle yet firm light.

Spectrum Academy gave me this possibility to provide for my family. I would be willing to live in the Layton Basement for one more year until I found something closer and what I could afford. I was motivated by the fact that Spectrum was going to provide financial stability. I would be, for the first time, in control of the money—a real living wage—how much was earned, and then what I could do to provide for the needs of my children and then hopefully to others.

It was the first real sign of hope; a SOLID pinpoint of light! It was like a flickering candle being held close to a wick of a firecracker that would soon rocket upward lighting our dark night with a flare of light to follow. Spectrum would rescue us from starving. It would supply my children's education and finally, it would give me motivation and purpose to stay focused for the safety of my children. This flare of light in the darkness was what I looked towards, as the darkest storm would yet unfold.

## CHAPTER 23

# Decisions: With the Inky Fog Lifted, I catch more Pinpoints of Light!

Decisions: the action or process of thinking about a choice between at least two options, or of resolving a question. Choices: making a decision based on at least two options. Decisions and choices happen throughout the day for everyone; around 35,000 conscious decisions per day. Making that many decisions a day can be mentally exhausting. However, like so many times in my life, the decisions that I was faced with during this time probably felt double to this number based on all the circumstances that we found ourselves in.

Choice and the *accountability* of our choices are the natural consequences and results of life. However, you do have power of choice. I had a choice to improve my family's life. My decision in 2005 to become a founding parent, then a board member, then a teacher at Spectrum Academy would improve the lives of my children. Going to school to receive my master's degree and teaching license would also improve their lives by giving them stability, and that's was what I choose to do.

Thanksgiving break gave me an opportunity to make a decision and have a choice in how I was going to respond based on the choices that were laid out in front of me. Thanksgiving, for me, signaled the start of celebrating with family throughout the next four weeks. I had Wednesday off—a rare treat—that lead to having a five-day weekend! I was going to fill this time with my children, cooking, going to a movie, and decorating for Christmas. I did all of that in checklist fashion and it felt wonderful! The four days of my five-day break was a needed break.

I knew that Thad was *not* going to be sober during the actual dinner of Thanksgiving because there would be a crowd: his half-siblings, his parents, and us. Therefore, I set my expectations for Thanksgiving Day by choosing *not* to base my hopes and my happiness for the holiday event on the idea that Thad could be sober for it. Remember, not a victim, but a victor! I accepted that he would be stoned or smashed, and I moved on with making a memory for the kids on that day. The feeling of freedom from THAT simple thought was freeing!

Thanksgiving was filled with family. It was filled with food, conversations, and I really enjoyed watching the children interact with their cousins. I watched them laugh and run around. I could see that they were living in the moment. They were enjoying the day. I was having a great time with game night and with talking with my sisters-in-law. Thad was there for dinner, but he was only there physically. His mind was buzzed with something and not too long following dinner, he left for hours. It was what I expected, so I was able to enjoy the day because I had already prepared myself that this was what was going to happen and to not wish for something else and end up disappointed.

True to our tradition, the day after Thanksgiving we hung up the Christmas decorations. We pulled out the three boxes of decorations, set up the tree, hung the stockings, and hung our lights. My children and I sat in the gentle basking glow of the tree and I told them family stories. The magical glow of Christmas lights held us in a feeling of hope that evening. I felt strengthened and knew that we had peace that night. I sat in a dream-like state in the magic of the lights for a good hour with my sleeping children. Then I lifted the children one by one off the couch and to their beds. I returned to the couch to sleep in the hope of those lights.

I felt so rested following that sleep. It was truly a refreshing sleep. As has been my habit of prayer, I was praying, talking, and thinking in the early morning hours on that Sunday while enjoying the lights of the tree. Suddenly, the clearest thought came in to my mind. It was a thought that I could feel. I knew that this thought and feeling was more than just a dream or any of my thoughts. I simply heard and felt, *"You have been released from your calling."*

I sat there in the lights of the Christmas tree, stunned by what I had felt. There was no doubt in my mind that I understood what that meant. I knew that my marriage was over. The nine plus years of the mental and emotional anguish of trying to make the marriage work was over. I had been released!

I felt a surge of feelings rush over me from excitement to peace. I knew that my life was going to be different, but that I would be free from the worrying about where Thad was, who he was with, what he was spending the money on, who he was going to hurt next, or if he was going to be found dead or alive somewhere. That was going to be over. He was going to be handed his freedom; the freedom he has wanted for a lifetime.

Since it was the Sabbath day, the children and I went to church. I enjoyed the first meeting with peace. The hymn that we sang in preparation to partake of the sacrament was about forgiveness and humility. My heart was touched to know that Jesus really could forgive everything. As the priests turned over the white cloth and began to break the bread, I felt a connection.

During the prayer over the bread, I *felt* the words that "we will *always* remember Him." I saw in my mind's eye the face of Jesus. I saw His kind eyes looking at me with such empathy and understanding. He really understood my pain from years; the abuse and neglect that we had suffered. He took that pain (loss, unwanted, unloved, hurt, manipulated, falling for lies, again and again, hoping for a different outcome) upon himself for me. I saw again His face so tenderly looking at me teaching me that this was not an event, but this was how he *LOVES* all of us.

As I partook of the bread all this understanding of love was given to me and wet tears splashed down my face. Jesus's love would help heal us. He would give us space and time away from the abuse to heal, but I must cling to the covenants I've made in order to bless the lives of my five children. I had to decide that. Leaving an abusive marriage did not mean I was leaving my covenants, but I was leaving the abuse to protect my children.

As the words of the prayer were said over the water, I also saw in my mind's eye Jesus then turning from us and reaching out towards Thad. He went to search for the lost sheep, for Thad. Jesus has the power to really do that. The Spirit gave me the understanding that Thad was in Jesus's care. That He loved him just as He loved me. He would protect us from the abuse, and still care for and heal Thad through time. He would work with Thad, and I was to go free.

As my lips touched the cup of water representing the blood of Christ's Atonement, I heard an understanding from the Spirit that He will continue to help Thad. I also felt that

I was to *let go and allow the Savior to save Thad*. I swallowed hard, feeling a gentle rebuke and yet understanding at the same time. I was not a savior. I needed to let go and allow the Savior to help Thad.

Tears burned down my face with that understanding. More and more confirmation was given to me that the marriage was over. I let the music wash over me. I felt the love of the talks, and I could feel my Savior's arms around me. I knew that I would not be alone on this journey. That my children and I would have Jesus by my side, and that Thad would too. We would all be watched over as we went our separate ways.

Finally, I knew in my heart that this was going to be the last Sunday I would have in this ward. I knew that I needed to talk to my bishop about my decision that I had made. Following the meeting, I found the Bishop walking in the hallway. I asked if he had a quick moment to meet with me. He could see my tear stained cheeks, said that he did, and we proceeded into his office.

I sat down, took a big breath, and looked him in the eye and told him I was getting a divorce. I was blunt. I did not mince words. The Bishop simply sat and nodded his head. I told him that I was going to give Thad his "freedom" and that I was going to be free as well. Free from the chaos and the abuse. He then said, "You know that it's right, so I will support you and your family." My Bishop never once asked me to reconsider, to take more time, or anything like that. I know that the Spirit confirmed to him, what I had felt that morning; that I had been released from my calling. I left that office feeling more and more peace. It was time to now face the hardest part. It was time to return home to tell Thad.

Upon returning from Church with the family, I found Thad at home just getting up from a hangover. I wanted to find a better time to tell him that I was done with the marriage—that I was going to divorce him. I wanted him to be able to understand the words and the impact when he was sober, not in his hangover state. However, I also knew that if I didn't tell him at that moment, I might not follow through with it. I was not going to wait any longer. I suddenly blurted out, "Thad, I am getting a divorce."

He just sat there on the bed. I told him again that I was divorcing him. He was still—sitting in a bit of fog and pain from the night but he seemed to understand. He was quiet at first and even sitting down. My words began to sink in following the third time I said it. After that third time, he started to stand up and took in some deep breaths as if he was stoking a fire.

As the concept started to penetrate deeper and deeper to him, he started pacing back and forth like a caged animal still taking in deep breaths. Finally, he had quickened his pacing, was wringing his hands till his knuckles turned white, and began shaking his head back and forth, yelling, "*No. No! NO!*" Then suddenly, he froze! His eyes lit up, turned and stared at me, and his expression dropped from rage to silence. He was still. Absolutely quiet.

Quiet silence filled the small hall space. The tension was palpable like a rubber band ready to snap! Then softly, he began to mumble. He began a conversation with someone, his *mind friends—John?* His expressions of words and with his face were hollow. His pacing slowly started up again and his mumbling continued.

I was not going to watch another temper tantrum and manipulation, so I turned away from the mumbling and pacing. I walked calmly into the kitchen to begin making Sunday dinner. I had done it! I had taken the first real step to end this madness! I was going to have some real time, some true peace!

As I was lifting out some pots and pans, like a flash Thad was right there, his fist pounding on the counter, and he was shouting, "You are not in control of me! I make the decisions! I am the boss! I am a ninja! You won't know where I strike!" I just looked at him with pity and with exhaustion. I was not going to be snagged by the old hooks or by the old habits of our relationship; ninja? Fine, now you are a ninja I thought. I had made my decision to end the marriage based on the truth I had learned that morning. I knew my answer and he was going to have to learn to accept it. He continued to pound his fist in three beat rhythms, and shouting threats. Suddenly, *I* slammed down the pot I had in my hand and looked at him with absolute resolve and shouted with strength, "If YOU try to do anything stupid, I will guarantee you won't see the children ever again!"

Those words escaped from my mouth, they seemed to hang in the air as if someone else had said them. They lingered there as the vapor of smoke after the final light of the candle has gone out. He was startled by my force and by my power!

> "If YOU try to do anything stupid, I will guarantee you won't see the children ever again!"

He turned his body towards the door, but his eye just glared at me as if to scan me for a weakness, then suddenly his eyes rolled following the direction of the rest of his body. He took five huge steps towards the door, grabbed his coat off the rusted hook, threw it on. He grasped the dull rough doorknob and flashed his red eyes in my direction one more time. "I am a ninja! I will strike at night!" He pulled open the door and left, slamming it behind him. I took a deep breath and turned back to my cooking.

I continued in my routine of Sunday so that I stayed focused. I knew Thad had left to do his drugs and be with his *mind friends*. I did not worry about it. I just focused on the routine. However, this Sunday afternoon to evening was not going to happen like my regular schedule at all. I had to make *decisions* about how I was going to respond to the intense events during the next seven hours of the darkest part of the night I would ever feel again. The next seven hours I have named, *That Night.*

## CHAPTER 24

# *That Night: The Hurricane that made Landfall*

Following dinner, I gathered the girls for their bath when suddenly Thad exploded back through the kitchen door in a very altered state. He was jumpy, with eyes flashing back and forth, and was breathing as if he had run a marathon. I ignored him. In fact, I even rolled my eyes and continued walking down the hallway and into the bathroom with the girls. I could hear that he was following me because of his heavy breathing, but I felt prompted to *ignore him*—this was going to be the same old manipulation—I was NOT going to fall for it! I turned on the water for the tub and talked with my girls as I undressed them. Thad's heavy breathing was louder and louder in the bathroom. Again, I was prompted to ignore him. I gently set the girls in the tub and kept my focus on them.

Thad had blocked the door to the bathroom with his body by spreading his legs across the entranceway and his arms were braced against the casing. From this position, he started yelling at me. "You can never take away my freedom!" Again, I ignored him. He wanted me to engage in his game—another mind game manipulation! NO! I shouted in my mind. I would no longer be a part of his sick game! I continued the wash their hair and hold their hands for reassurance that "mommy was here for them."

He pounded his fist on the door jam and shouted it again. "You can never take away my freedom!" I never looked at him. I never engaged him. All I could think was that Thad's yelling was going to bring my father-in-law downstairs in to the mess. I did not look back at Thad. Then, his heavy breathing started up again. It was like the sound from a bellows for a fire. "I am a Ninja and I will strike at night!" Suddenly, I could see the fear in my girls' eyes as they heard the words continue to fly out of his mouth. He was very loud and my girls reached out for me. One thought flashed in my mind, *he could drown the girls—get them out!*

A surge of adrenaline and fear flooded my veins, and I quickly took them out of the water and wrapped them in towels. I suddenly saw how trapped I was. Thad continued pounding on the door jam, blocking my path to get out of the bathroom. He was screaming, "I am the Ninja and will STRIKE at night!" He repeated that three times when suddenly Thad changed—in a flash, he switched from rage to calm. My heart started racing more and a trickle of sweat ran down my back.

> *I willed my frantic heart to not give away my fear.*

I willed my frantic heart to not give away my fear. His mind friends had control and now I would be fighting more than just Thad.

Thad released his grip on the door jam, took a deep breath, and started a conversation with his mind friend, John, about the next construction project that was coming up. He acted as if he had been meeting with a client and his body language changed from focusing rage towards me to nearly open and relaxed. He had released the grip on the doorway and had turned his body three-quarters of the way around as if heading to the bedroom down the hall. He just kept talking to himself. I saw how his own mind friends distracted him, and I took advantage of it scooting the girls past Thad's turned body and into the hallway.

As I slipped past him, in a flash he turned back around, grabbed my arm, and twisted it up under my neck, which picked me off the floor slamming me in to the wall. I gasped for breath— My feet were off the ground, and I was eye level with him. He kept shaking/slamming me against the wall whispering fiercely with spit flying in my face. "You are going to pay!"

I was sucking in air as the pressure mounted against my throat, when suddenly, just as before, the rage in his eyes vanished. He released his grip, and the choking pressure was off of my throat. I slide down the wall gasping for air hoping that my windpipe would open up again.

As I hit the floor gasping and coughing, I turned to see my girls still in their towels looking at me with their crying eyes. My son Garrett was there with his eyes wide open with fear on his face. Thad was just a few feet from them. He turned back to look at me as I fought my way back to my feet. I had to get between Thad and the kids. Thad turned back from me and towards the kids. This was all happening so fast, yet the feeling was in slow motion. Thad glared at the three children and then spit at Garrett. Thad suddenly shifted, turned away from the kids, and strutted in to the bedroom.

Garrett started to scream and cry. I staggered and reached out for Garrett grabbing him close and hugged him. I whispered to him, "Let's rock. Rock time?" It was hard to talk and catch my breath, but I fought through the pain to say those distracting words for my children. My girls were whimpering and gathered around me as I was comforting Garrett. With my body, I turned this little group down the hallway and towards the girl's room to get them dressed. Thoughts were running through my head: keep calm this will pass. My heart was racing and saying the opposite; I needed to get help! How? More fear was rising—you have work tomorrow; you can't miss—you'll lose your job! Get help! I was in a tug of war with what to do.

It was with that fear that I herded my little group into the living room where Isaac was bouncing on the mini trampoline. Another thought hit me; *you will know when to get help.* I gently placed Garrett in the rocking chair. I gave him his bear. He started rocking/slamming his back against the chair in his autistic stimming pattern of comfort. Once he found his rhythm, I told him that I would be back. Isaac continued to pound up and down on the tramp, and I directed the girls into their room.

In the bedroom, I gathered diapers, combs, and pajamas and sat on the ground with both girls. Virginia was still wrapped snugly in her towel, and I started helping Margaret. I put on her diaper, soft pajamas and gently brushed her long blonde hair. Margaret was finished. I placed her in her bed when suddenly; Thad appeared again in the doorway of their room. His goofy drug-warped grin split across his face. Tap, tap, tap was the sound of his nails on the doorframe. Then with two giant steps, he was in the room. I quickly picked up Virginia, and in my rush, she had started crying.

I began walking and rocking her. Thad followed me around the room as I tried to rock Virginia. He was behind me whispering, "You'll never win! I am never going to lose!" His high-pitched whispered laughter was right behind the words.

He was at my neck. I could feel the hot hatred in his breath as he was nearly biting my neck as he kept saying the words.

My heart started thundering in my chest and fear was rising and rising like a panicked swimmer. *Don't engage him—he wants to suck you in to his darkness! You must keep calm.* I clung to that prompting like a lifeline. With shaking arms, I clung to my daughter and ignored him. Finally, he turned and walked out of the room, and I soon heard the kitchen door slam shut behind him again. Deep breath... let the tension go was the next thought. Keep going.

I quickly laid Virginia down diapered and slipped on her pajamas. I lifted Margaret out of her bed and I gathered the Virginia in to the rocking chair. I tried to distract them by reading them a story. Virginia still had soft whimpers but seemed to be settling. I rocked and rocked both of them as I read. The soothing rocking motion was calming for all of us and soon they fell asleep in the safety of my arms. Once asleep, I lifted them into their beds and quietly shut the door. *Run! Now is your chance get help! Go!* I thought.

As I turned from the door, I was met with Isaac. He looked nervous; different. I picked him up and walked into the living room. He never said anything, but he was scared. I looked for Garrett, but he was not in the chair. Suddenly I realized how quiet it all was. With Isaac in my arms, I ran through my bedroom and back to the boy's room when I heard Garrett scream.

Upon opening up the door I caught my breath! Thad was in the room! How? He had left! Now, he was back—I NEVER heard the door open! My eyes focused on Thad with his back to me. He was standing behind my son Kellis who was sitting on a chair. Thad was holding Kellis's shoulder down with one hand. He was holding the barrel of our shotgun vertical toward the ceiling. Fear gripped my body, as my head shouted—not the gun! Not the gun! I stood frozen, yet my heart was hammering against my chest. *Don't scream—that will fuel his rage!* came the voice with steadying force. Thad heard me come in, and his grip turned knuckle white around the barrel. He took a deep breath and he turned towards me and released the hold on Kellis's shoulder. Thad's face had split in to another crazed grin.

I stood there, in the doorway, with Isaac in my arms, looking at Thad's rage rising. My heart was panicking! Kellis had turned his head with fear looking at me from the chair, and Garrett screaming on his bed. Thad marched towards me with heavy thudding steps, lifting the shotgun up to his head screaming, "I will be FREE!!" No! I was screaming in my head! No! *Stay calm* the voice warned sharply. Then Thad turned back around and aimed the gun toward Garrett. He turned and aimed toward Kellis. He turned again and aimed toward Isaac who was in my arms. Thad quickly then lifted the gun to side his own head. No. No! I was shouting in my head.

Thad's crazed terror filled the room of our little boys and I had no power to stop this! My fear had frozen me again allowing my children to be terrorized. With a flash of his eyes, he looked at me and I had to act fast but keep calm. I was standing at the doorway, blocking it. Thad had the gun still pointed at his own head. I stepped aside opening the pathway for Thad, and said, "Your freedom, Mr. Jefferson!" The Spirit put those words there, and they clicked with Thad.

He dropped the gun from his head, but it was still in his grasp! His eyes were flickering from left to right rapidly, raging. With a jerk of his head, he flashed his eyes opened. He ran towards the door shouting, "FREEDOM!" He ran past me down the hallway, through the kitchen, and slammed the door shut for a third time that evening.

Silence echoed from the slamming door and seemed to spread towards us like a fast rolling fog. All was quiet. All was calm. *Breathe,* the familiar prompting said. *Calm! You must help your family to remain calm,* for the third time that night. I was gripping Isaac so tightly just to help control my shaking body.

> *Silence echoed from the slamming door and seemed to spread towards us like a fast rolling fog.*

As I turned to look back at the boys again, Kellis was still staring at me, and Garrett had stopped screaming. I was still holding Isaac. As silence echoed through the room, I knew I needed to shatter it and get the boys distracted and feeling loved. I took all my energy to silence my fears and focus on them. This was when autism was a blessing. I was able to use the power of distraction to change the subject and feeling of what had just happened. I saw a book on the floor to the side of me, reached down and picked it up and asked, "Who wants a story?" It just happened to be one of their favorite books.

Kellis got to his bed first. I put Isaac down on his bed and I read the book in an animated fashion. Even Garrett occasionally turned from his stimming of flapping his hands to participate in the reading. It was an Oscar-winning performance. I used a variety of voices for the characters and rubbed my boy's legs as I read to them. They were distracted by the story and looked peaceful. It had worked. *Just keep calm and help them feel peace* came the feeling throughout the entire time I was with them. We said prayers and no one mentioned anything that had happened. We had to take the moment we created and live there.

I walked out of the room with my back towards the door and with my face still facing my boys. I smiled at them and told them that I loved them. I then reached for the doorknob, stepped back into the hallway, and pulled the door shut with a final click. I rested my forehead against the door. I took my first real deep breath. I took huge breaths, holding them and slowly releasing them. I continued to hold my shaky grip on to the doorknob while I took in three more breaths to try to calm myself.

Now that the children were in their rooms and quiet, I had to take a few moments to think. I started making a list of what I knew: 1) Thad was in an altered state of mind—amplified by whatever drug he was on. 2) His mind friends were very active and telling Thad that he had no control. One answer came in to my head, *it was time to get help—lock him out! Go now!*

The thought about Thad having no control repeated in my mind. I must lock him out! I took a final breath, and I released my grip on the door, and turned around to run and lock the door, but instead was to face my father-in-law.

I jumped back against the door with a start. My father-in-law? What was he doing here? What? Really? Now? This was like a nightmare that never ends! I was just trying to get a grip on the reality of being threatened with my life, and now I had to face my father-in-law? He didn't even say hi.

He plowed in to the same monologue that he always did after he had heard one of our fights. He was blocking my way. I needed to lock the door! He said that he understood that things had been tough. He started spewing the list of all our failures and then said that we should NOT jump to divorce. I was trying to get past him to lock the door, but he kept blocking the hallway.

He repeated that he could help calm Thad and help him run the business again. He was going to be there for him, help Thad clean up, and on and on. I've heard this speech hundreds of times since Thad and I have been married.

Finally, I saw a gap, I pushed past him running through the kitchen, to the door. I grabbed the lock and twisted the bolt, click—the door was locked! I backed away from the locked door looking at that small inch of metal. *He doesn't have a key!* It will at least give me a warning. Suddenly my ears picked up the words from my father-in-law—he was still going on and on! I turned and started cleaning up the kitchen. He took that social clue to mean, "I guess she didn't hear me, so I'll keep going."

My mind was listing ways to leave, who to call for help, how to get away from Thad while I cleaned, and while my father-in-law's voice kept blathering on. I had to pretend that I was listening to him. I could not tell him of the violence that had happened. Why? He would blame me for the violence—*for not loving Thad enough.* That *if I would be a better wife, then Thad wouldn't stay away from home and do drugs.* No! He had betrayed me before. I did NOT trust him.

I knew what I was going to do. This divorce was happening, and my father-in-law's speech was not going to change it. He continued to pontificate. Throughout this speech, he was right about one thing; Thad needed help. He needed to get clean. He needed to start over. But where this lecture ended was the fact that he would not have me on the other side of it. Thad was going to have to do all those things without the kids or me.

He must have finally run out of words. I could feel him staring at me, and I was not going to meet his gaze. He finally turned and left. I put down the final pan in to the drying rack. I forced myself to breathe deeply for a few minutes in the quiet of the kitchen with the scent of soap, which lingered in the air, to settle myself so that I could rest. Monday was in a few hours, and the crushing week schedule would start up again. I reached up and felt the skin on my throat. The mark was going to be visible. I would have to take care of that tomorrow.

I felt exhausted because there was so much going on that it was all catching up with me now, and Monday was racing closer; it was nearing midnight. We are safe for the night. *The door was locked.* He won't return tonight—I hoped. As I undressed, my mind went to all the events throughout the night, and I was turning them over and over again: thoughts of Thad potentially drowning the girls, of me being slammed against the wall and choked, him yelling "I am a ninja! I will strike at night!" Him yelling "freedom," the shotgun being pointed at my children, at him, at me, and those crazed eyes: the eyes of fear, rage, hatred, and craziness!

I finished pulling on my pajamas and collapsed in to bed. I listened to the stillness of that night. There was no more noise, no more words, no more yelling, and no more mind friends. I was just still and somewhere in that stillness, I slipped in to the gray fog of a dreamless sleep.

Gray. Was it light, a color, or was it a feeling of craziness? It was gray and dark. It looked like a mix of either dawn or twilight. I couldn't distinguish between them. Was it time to wake up, or had I just fallen asleep? The light remained the same for what seemed like forever. It was neither day nor night. I was just stuck ... I decided to roll over when my eyes shot awake because my skin felt cold steel against it.

I saw the silhouette of Thad, and the cold steel blade of a knife pressed against my neck as his hand clenched around the handle. His smoky breath fell across my face, "I will have my FREEDOM!" He pressed the flat side of the metal blade against my neck again, "I am the Ninja and I will strike at night!" His breathing was steady and hot. How did he get in? The lock! I know I locked it!

My heart was beating fast across the cold blade of his knife. It was bound to give me away—I was no longer calm! Thad's hands held the cold steel knife against my skin and with the slightest pressure, with the slightest movement, he could take my life—he was in full control!

He held me there while time seemed to be suspended; it was neither dawn nor dusk. My heart kept pounding across the cold blade. *Just keep calm* I was prompted for a ninth time that night. I trusted that prompting and forced down my fear! I lay there with a knife blade pressed against my neck and did not respond. I did not give him a clue of my fear. My heart banging against my ribs seemed undetected by him. I kept my breathing as quiet as possible. I simply laid still. While the whole time his breathing was labored and unsteady. He was waiting for me to cry out, to move, to fight back, but I was still.

Suddenly, he released the pressure of the blade and slowly stood over me. My feet began to sweat—was he going to lunge? His shaking breathing was labored. He still pointed the knife toward me. "*Freedom!*" he hissed as he backed out of the room and through the doorway. Then he paused and fiercely whispered, "*Freedom!*" one last time. Once again, the sound of the footsteps led toward the kitchen door. I heard the click of the bolt, doorknob turn and the door open. The sound of the heavy door shutting back in the frame, the handle clicking in to place ended the darkest night of my life: Sunday, November 26th, 2006.

# CHAPTER 25

# Eye of the Storm: False Hope Brings Reprieve

I woke with a sudden jolt! My eyes flashed to the clock 6:48 am. Late! Late! I flew out of bed running around the room trying to find direction from the chaos of last night. We had made it through *that night*! It was now Monday, and I was late for our routine, school, and work!

The checklist began to pour out of my head, and verbally out of my mouth to help me organize my thoughts. 12 minutes to put the kids in the car, get ready for work, and drive. This was not going to happen! But I had to be at work! I couldn't lose my job. I couldn't let go of the only stability in my life—especially following last night! I threw on my sweater and jumped in to my pants, pulled on my left shoe, as soon as I place my foot in the right shoe I was frozen in place. The Spirit was very direct, *No work today.*

Monday, November 27th was not going to be a work day. All I could think of was my classroom, the students, and my job? Firmly the Spirit repeated, *no work today*. I picked up my phone and sent a text to my boss, and my paraprofessional that I was not coming in, but that I would be back tomorrow. My hands were shaking as I texted that. I subconsciously rubbed my neck where his hands and his blade lay last night to calm my hand.

Sending that text was a frightening thing for me to do. I felt more fear with doing that then from what I experienced the night before. How could that be? I knew that it was irrational to think that if I missed one day of work then I would be fired, but this was more than missing one day of work.

I put the phone down and sat back on my bed. I just sat and thought of nothing but of being free. My heart seemed to smile, I felt very alive on this Monday morning and I felt peace. We had made it through a dangerous night and in to the peaceful morning: all of us. As the children woke from their slumber, I shared with them that we were going to just enjoy the day. My children were thrilled to have one more day home with me.

The sun was actually shining that chilly November day, so we went outside and jumped on the trampoline. I bounced with them and wrestled and enjoyed their laughter. From there, we came back into the basement and I thought, I *do NOT* want to stay here. Where could we spend more time out in the sun? The idea came to have a picnic. I packed a quick lunch and we drove to the park. We had our lunch, fed the ducks, and played at the playground. We just relaxed. I watch the warm rays of sunlight warm my children as they laughed and played on the merry-go-round. I watched the light bounced off their faces and they rocked and soared back and forth on the swings. I also watched the warm rays begin to lose their strength as they tipped and dipped towards the western sky.

With the warmth of the light gone and the cold creeping in, we found ourselves heading for home. As the sun began to dip in to the west, my thought of never seeing this place again struck my mind. I was caught off guard by that thought because my mind had lived in the moment of this day. I had captured the smiles on my children's faces in my heart. I had simply lived in the joy of this healing day. However, the short day was ending, and it was time to return to the underground and prepare for tomorrow. Our day in the sun had ended, and it had been filled with light.

As I was working in the kitchen with the children, Thad returned home. His footsteps in the garage signaled that he was home. He gripped the metal knob, turned it, and came inside. There was a rush of cold air, as he turned to close the door. He pushed it shut with a soft click. He was calm. He stood near the washer and dryer. Not daring to come any closer. His tired eyes kept looking at me. He kept searching for me to look back at him. Finally, I did and gave him a look that I told him that the divorce was still happening. He returned the look, and walked toward the kitchen table, slid in a chair. He looked at me again. It was the *real* Thad actually looking at me. He was there. It wasn't his *mind friends* or his drugs. He had pain in his eyes, but not manipulative pain; it was real pain.

He turned as the children came to the table. He looked around at all of them, at the four walls in the kitchen, and then back at me. He said, "I'm sorry. I'm sorry that I've ruined us. I'm so far gone, that I don't know how to return."

*My worn green eyes looked at his aged blue eyes and I think for the first time in seven or eight years we just saw each other.*

My worn green eyes looked at his aged blue eyes and I think for the first time in seven or eight years we just saw each other. That was the first honest thing that Thad had said to me in eight years. It was deep. It was emotional for me.

I was shaken by the cry of Virginia. She had spilled her milk and it was running onto her lap. I was surprised by the

156

smile on my face. Thad and I, together, helped to clean her up; I was surprised at this gesture of kindness. It was random, but it was real. My eyes again looked at his and his were swimming with tears, and I realized my emotion did not spill down my face but stirred deep in my heart and to my bones. I hadn't thought about Thad being kind, gentle, or loving in years. My mind kept replaying how we started out, our potential, and now to see us back here in the basement for a final time together understanding that it was over; it was tragic but right.

As we finished cleaning up Virginia, he looked at all the children around the table, and held their gaze with each one. Time was quieted and stilled; it seemed to hang right there long enough for him to say he was sorry to each one of us. He looked back and I accepted that this was going to happen; it was over. He was just normal, calm. His eyes reached back to mine, and I painfully turned away and continued finishing dinner.

We ate around the table together. Together, without him being stoned, but being sober. I said a prayer over the meal and hoped that we could just enjoy this moment in time. Following the prayer, food passed, reminders to use forks, reminders to wipe, chew with mouth closed etc. commenced. We sat together we ate together, and for once in a long time, we were all around the table as a family. We talked about the fun of the day, and we just felt normal. He connected, he laughed, we enjoyed this moment, but I knew that it was only going to be a moment. However, it was the right way to say goodbye. It was the *real* Thad that I had known nine years before, but many of our children had never really met. Thad was with us for this small blip of time.

There was a pang of sadness in my heart that this dinner, our last together, would soon end. As the last bite of food was taken and the silverware placed back on the table, the magic of the moment had ended. It was time for the bedtime routine. Thad got up from the table and smiled one more smile at each of us. He looked at me one more time and said he was sorry. He slowly walked the two or three steps to the door, gently grasped the metal knob, twisted it, and opened the door to walk out. He turned one more time. I saw *him* for the last time that night, and the door shut with a soft click. That was it. It was a calm and quiet night much different than the night before.

Last night, *That Night*, we had been in a storm—a hurricane! The winds of fear and anxiety were blowing at their height last night. The choking feeling of pain returned to my memory as I tried to swallow. Last night he held me at my neck two different times. The symbolic rage of the ocean crashing against my little children was like Thad's altered state that mocked and laughed at their fear. *That Night* held the power of the wind and it never stopped, until the morning came. The Calm. The Quiet. This day we found ourselves in the eye of the storm. Sunlight, warmth, time to play, time to live in the moment and a time to say goodbye had now passed. I took a quick sharp breath as I lay in bed knowing that the backside of the storm was yet to come.

# CHAPTER 26

# The Arrest: A Glimmer of Hope sliced through the Shadow

That cold Tuesday, November 28, 2006, started out as any other: wake up, hurry the children in to their clothes, pour cereal in sandwich sacks, pack the lunches, made sure everyone had socks, shoes, backpacks, and coats. I whisked everyone in to the car by 7:15 am in the morning. Drive, unload the girls at the daycare—hugs and kisses a tug of guilt, but they are cared for—I was doing the best I could. I drove the rest of us to Spectrum Academy and started the teaching day. Normal right? This was the routine and had been since September 11, 2006, so why would the 28th of November be any different?

The workday went as planned: morning check-in, review the visual schedule, teach reading, morning recess, teach writing, go to lunch, story time, math time, then social studies, afternoon recess, the closure of the day. Take a bathroom break, clean up, and ready for carpool. I had planned for sensory breaks, for meltdowns, classroom management, and behavioral interventions for nineteen children who had autism and that was simultaneously happening with the academic teaching. It was rewarding and exhausting.

Tick, Tick, Tick.... Ding! It was the end of the day. Time for Carpool! Carpool was normally a small celebration that signified I had made it through another day—check! However, about 10 minutes before school let out, I notice my father-in-law walking (well kind of stumbling down the long hallway) towards my room. Since it was Tuesday, the fact that my father-in-law was there to pick up my children was not unusual. Tuesday was the night I went to my master's program. I had made arrangements with my in-laws to exchange cars, pick up the children, and care for them on the night I had class. We had been doing this for three months. However, what was unusual was the fact that he was not in the van waiting in the carpool line. He was in the building, walking, and stumbling in pain, towards my room.

I asked my paraprofessional to prep the class for carpool so that I could talk to my father-in-law out in the hall. When our eyes met, I knew that whatever the story was, it was going to involve Thad. I asked him what was wrong, and he told me a story that was nearly unbelievable.

A few weeks prior to Thanksgiving, Thad's Toyota truck had died on him. Thad had been trying to figure out ways to fix it, but with no access to the money I was making, he was flat broke. Thad knew it was time to pick up the kids and so he begged my father-in-law to take him down to the school so that he could talk to me. He hesitated, but eventually, he let him come down with him.

During their drive, they had gotten in to a fight. They were talking about all the events on Sunday night and it caused Thad to freak out! Thad's temper and altered state, *mind friends* had flared up again. Thad grabbed a hammer that was in the back seat of the car and threatened to hit him with a hammer while they were driving. He stopped the car and Thad attacked him hitting him with the hammer. Then, he shoved his dad out of the driver's seat onto the busy intersection and drove off.

My father-in-law was disoriented and dazed because of the blow to his head. He slowly got up off the road and out of the intersection to the safety of the sidewalk. He said that once he was off the road, the only thing he could think to do was to walk towards the school. He was hurt and injured, but he needed to get to the school to come and tell me the story—the whole story.

In the hallway at the school, he explained to me what happened to him Sunday night. He had been trying to rest but with the noise of our fight, he was not able to let go of the thoughts that gripped him. He closed his eyes and must have dozed off because he shot awake to dark shadow that hung over him. It was Thad holding a knife to his throat whispering fiercely that he was "not going to let anyone take his freedom!"

Thad kept repeating "...not going to let anyone take his freedom" phrase over and over again. He tried to talk and reason with him. Thad lunged and stepped forward as the debate continued. He held the knife to my father-in-law for over 20 minutes Sunday night. My mouth was pulled tight as he recalled the night. My father-in-law just kept shaking his head in disbelief as the words fell from his mouth. My eyes were wide with shock! I subconsciously reached under my scarf and touched the side of my neck where the cold steel had creased against my skin on the same night.

> *I subconsciously reached under my scarf and touched the side of my neck where the cold steel had creased against my skin on the same night.*

My mind quickly started checking off the "to do" list and solutions to assess the situation and figure out what my next move was: 1) father-in-law's car was gone, 2) he was injured, and 3) I had to get to my master's program. I was jolted out of my thoughts by the school's PA system! Suddenly children's names are being called out for carpool, and the hallway was busy and filled with movement.

As he continued to talk about the events, children began filling in the hallways because of the carpool. All this is happening when I suddenly looked out the glass doors in to the parking lot. My van was gone! What was going on? More and more children, names over the PA, and in the chaos or carpool, I told my father-in-law to wait for me and I ran down the hallway and outside to the parking lot desperately looking for my van!

My van was nowhere! Suddenly around the carpool lane, the police pulled into the parking lot with lights flashing. The problems of my life were now slowly unraveling and spilling out in to public! I didn't understand who had called them because no one knew that my van was missing. I ran back in to the building and towards my father-in-law, but a coworker intercepted me. She was asking me what was going on? What could she do to help? I asked her to get my three kids and keep them distracted, and to wait for me while I tried to find answers to this crazy afternoon!

I went back to find my father-in-law and he was speaking with one of the officers. As I stepped closer I could hear the officer say they had responded to a 911 call that led them to this school. The officer said that three people had reported a road rage innocent resulting in a man being thrown out of a car in a busy intersection and that man started stumbling towards this school. (They had just described my father-in-law's event).

Since there were two officers, one took his statement while the other talked to me. The officer began asking questions about Thad and if I knew any more about the attack. I shared with him all that I knew from what he had told me. I interrupted the story by adding that my van had been stolen! The officer took the information and added it to this strange attack and left to talk to his partner.

I walked towards my father-in-law. He kept shaking his head and saying that he wasn't sure what to do. He was debating if he *should* or *shouldn't* press charges against his own son. He kept shaking his head in disbelief that he had to make a decision like this. My mind kept flipping from the reality in the hallway, trying to solve what was going to be my next move in this unpredictable, unstable, life.

Then suddenly at that moment, an answer came. It was a ray of light slicing through the dark storm. I looked at him, right in the eye and said, *"press charges* against Thad." He stopped his debate and looked back at me. I said with conviction, "A few days in jail will help him to sober up! It will keep us all safe!" Again, my words hung out there in the air like a bubble. My father-in-law clung to the words *safe* and *sober*, and repeated them to himself a few more times, *safe* and *sober*. He looked back at me and said he agreed to press the charges.

Once he had decided that, he approached the officer and started the process. I took the spare moment to run and check on my kids to see if there were safe and hopefully CLUELESS about what was taking place on the other side of the door. Affirmative on both accounts: safe, and clueless—phew! I walked back to the principal's office to finish talking with the officers about my van. The second officer had been able (through backup support) to find my stolen van. They found my father-in-law's car and Thad! This news was like winning the lottery!

I asked the officer how this happened, and he explained that Thad picked up someone off the street, told him he would pay him some money if he drove my van and follow him. The guy agreed; they drove to the school "stole" the van and drove off. They didn't get far because my van was nearly out of gas, so they stopped at the gas station at the intersection where the attack on my father-in-law had taken place.

As they drove out of the station they had headed in the direction of the school, and a fourth police officer who had just been called to the scene saw the description of the two stolen vehicles as there were on the same street 100 yards from the school. I couldn't believe our blessings! All of the prayers that had been going on in my heart that day were being answered directly. I thanked the officer for his fast work. There was a knock on the doorframe. It was his partner. He called him out of the office to finish up the business of the day, and I found myself alone with all the events and thoughts spinning through my head.

What had all transpired was like a nightmare: fast, dangerous, crazy events swirled together and compressed in to mere minutes! I was deep in prayerful thoughts when a flash of movement through the blinds caught my eye. I looked through the slits in the blinds of the principal's office to the scene that was unfolding outside. Thad was being handcuffed. He gave no resistance to the arrest, and in fact, he was eerily calm. I even saw him start to smirk at the police officer. That smirk, that looks of "you will pay for this" split across his face with a slight high-pitched laugh, and he turned and looked in the direction of the school and met my eyes through the blinds!

My fingers slipped off the blinds and I sank into the chair, my heart pounding against my ribs. My eyes just told me that Thad was not going to stay in jail—he was going to make bail and get out! From the scene of eerier calm that I just witnessed, if I stayed just one more night, we were going to be a news story later that night. This was it! I was leaving Thad, tonight!

I took a few deep breaths because the reality of that decision was overwhelming me with a thousand questions that had no answers. My thoughts: I don't know how to do this! I don't even know legally what I need to do first! I have no direction in protecting myself from harm!

I said all of that in my heart as one of my continued prayers because I had NO idea of how to make my next move, other than I was not going to be a victim for one more night.

I took another breath to calm myself and walked out of the principal's office and in to the hallway. I took another deep breath and told my father-in-law to keep it like any other Tuesday night. He would dive the kids home, get pizza, and I would go to school.

My heart was continuing to pray as I raced out the door of the school and towards the car when I noticed that there was still a police officer in the parking lot. He saw me and began approaching me. I was putting my things in the car when he started talking to me. He said that the arrest had been made and that Thad was going to be very busy for the next four to five hours as he was going to be booked in to the county jail. I thanked him for the information and fully expected him to turn and leave, but he didn't.

Instead, the officer turned again and said he felt like he needed to give me something. He handed me a card, a small simple business card. Then he looked at me long and hard. He said I needed to call the number on that card to help me obtain a protective order.

He looked at me again this time even more seriously and said: "whatever I decided to do, I would need to call that number so that if I did take the kids I would be able to run without being in trouble for kidnapping." My heart skipped, how did he know? My stomach lurched at the information that the officer had given me. I saw in my mind's eye that ray of light again slicing through the confusing questions of what to do, and I felt pulled to follow that light.

165

Again, for a third time, I saw that ray of light—enlightenment—penetrating the darkness of confusion and lead me to the faith that I could make this next move. I looked at the officer and thanked him. I knew what I needed to do. I had a legal way of getting away from Thad. This was another pinpoint of light! I knew that I was never going back.

CHAPTER 27

# Escape: Leaving it all Behind

To escape means: to flee, to leave, to run from, to get out, to exit, to vamoose, to never come back. Escapes can be narrow, and escapes are usually from danger. Our escape, November 28, 2006, was the pinpoint that took us in to the unknown.

I again thanked the officer, turned, opened my car door and sat in my car. Making this phone call was a real commitment to leaving the marriage behind and would change my life forever. I glanced at the clock, 3:52 pm. I noted that I had about one hour to make this all work before class started. I took a deep breath and dialed the number. My heart was pumping with adrenaline, which caused my hands to shake.

First ring…second ring…third ring…fourth ri—it went to the voicemail. *This is it! Leave the message* I was prompted. I said what the officer had explained to me to say making sure that I stated the date and time for the record. I took the phone from my face and with my shaking hands, pushed the end button. Step one done, and a million more to go. *Breathe! Breathe!* My trembling hands turned the key starting the engine and then I grasped the wheel for support as I drove out of the school's parking lot. My thoughts and heart were in continuous prayer that didn't stop for hours following that phone call.

I started the traffic-filled drive to class. It was time for step two: calling my Bishop, my friends, and Thad's half-sister explaining to them the events of the afternoon. The purpose of my phone calls was to warn them about how unstable Thad's mental health had become and why he was in jail. I emphasized to my sister-in-law that Thad had threatened us with guns, he had choked me, held me with a knife, and did the same to my father-in-law.

I knew that my mother and father-in-law needed protection from Thad while he was in this altered state. That smirk and the eerie calmness Thad displayed during the arrest told me that when he got out of jail that he was going to take that anger and rage and really hurt someone this time and not just threaten them but really follow through with these actions.

The miles on the road seemed to slip by as I continued to call everyone on the list and drive towards class. I then called my Bishop. My conversation with my Bishop was very direct. He understood the potential gravity of the situation. I told him that I needed one thing from him: I needed him to call me the minute he heard that Thad had posted bail. He agreed and then asked me what my plan was. I told the Bishop that I was leaving Thad that night and that I was not going to tell anyone where I was going to keep my children and myself safe. He asked if I had enough money to get through this next little while, and I told him that I was going to make it and do the best I could as long as I continued to follow the guidance of the Spirit. He promised that he would contact me; I thanked him, and then hung up the phone.

Suddenly, I was in my night class. I parked as close to the building as possible so that I could leave in a moment's notice. I said one more prayer for my children at home—that I would reach them before harm did. From that amen to the next amen, I'm not sure when it ever happened. Thoughts of how to run and where to go continually popped in to my mind, so my prayers seemed to continue on through the night.

I ran to the building for class, again, thinking and praying that with every step I would know how to handle class. I was in a program that required full attendance for five hours a night one time a week for a six-week class without missing a class. If I missed class, I would have to repeat the entire six-week course again. If it had been an eight-week rotation, then I would have been allowed to miss one class.

Unfortunately, in order to get credit, I must attend all five hours in order for the teacher to give me credit. This was not going to happen for me that night. Therefore, I knew I was going to have to pull my professor aside and tell her my circumstances. I had no idea how she was going to respond. I prayed that I could sign the attendance sheet as early as possible as opposed to at 10:00 that night. I explained to her that I was going to be receiving a phone call and upon receiving that call; I would immediately have to leave class for the safety of my family. I asked her not to press me for the details just that we were in some danger, and that I needed to leave as soon as that phone call came in.

She listened and when I said the word *danger*, she faced me. She gave me a short nod, and then she reached in to her bag, pulled out the attendance sheet for the night and had me sign it. That was it. I looked back at her hoping she could see my sense of gratitude and relief! I was still going to receive full credit! I was still going to be on track to finish! I was bound and determined to complete my coursework no matter what else came from the consequences of the past few weeks. I was so relieved. I thanked her so much and walked into class. I thanked the sweet Lord for that first of many continuous miracles.

I sat down and right away, my learning team could see that something was wrong but there was no time to talk. The class had started. I needed to pay attention and get what I could out of the class in order to pass it. I had to remain focused on the class and my plan. I could say something to them at our break. One hour down, then 30 minutes more; the first ten-minute break.

Suddenly my learning team turned to me asking tons of questions! How could I answer anything? Where would I start? How would I even begin? My learning team knew that I had five children, three had autism, but my focus had been on talking about my charter school, never about my husband.

I took another deep breath and gave them an answer in four summary sentences: 1) My husband was bipolar/schizophrenic and was an addict. 2) He was in a manic rage and had been violent against his family members over the past 72 hours. 3) He had been arrested but would post bail tonight. And 4) once I receive the call that bail has been posted, I would race home, gather my children, and run away. The last word bounced into the hallway as an echo. Some on my team were quiet, some had millions of more questions, but the break was over, and it was time to get back to class. We plowed on through class. Tick, tick, tick, 15 minutes had passed. Tick, tick, tick, 30 minutes had passed...ten more minutes, then suddenly, the phone rang.

I gathered my notebook and bag and began running to the door—ring two. I pushed the door opened—ring three! As the door fell shut behind me, I answered, "Hello?" It was my Bishop, "he posted bail. He is out." My eyes flashed with fear, and my stomach dropped! My hands started shaking because the adrenaline was pumping.

I ran to the elevator doors, punched the button, and the doors slid open. I punched the level one and the doors slid shut. Four... three... two... one... with a soft jerk, the elevator stopped and once again the doors slid open in to the lobby. I walked quickly—with a great purpose—out of the lobby. I was panting and breathing in a shallow manner. The icy wall of air that hit me as I shoved open the heavy glass doors and raced in to the darkness towards the car.

My breath was like little steam clouds pumping from my mouth as I ran in the frigid cold. My thoughts were tumbling around in my head, talking to me, coaching me so I listened: *It's time.... time to leave! Drive, April, just drive. Get home, get the things, place the kids in the van one at a time...just be quiet! Be QUIET!*

> *It's time.... time to leave! Drive, April, just drive. Get home, get the things, place the kids in the van one at a time... just be quiet! Be QUIET!*

It was tough to unlock the door with so much adrenaline pumping through me. I got the key in, unlocked the door, threw my bags in, then started the car. Fumbling with the buckle I clicked it in to place, grasped hold of the steering wheel, turned the key, pull out, and took off. Soon, ten miles had gone by, and then twenty miles were down, then another five miles. Through the frozen night, I flew. I saw my exit, my road, same street, the green light flashed from the signal. I made the left turn down the winding road, down the hill—to my children!

As soon as I came to the driveway, I turned off the headlights, coasted down the long driveway. I was here! I was at the Basement! I quietly parked my father-in-law's car on the backside of the house. I noticed that my van had been parked in the garage. I turned off the engine. Silence. I reached back and grabbed my bags. I opened the door to the car and stepped out into the night. My cold breath came out as a cloud as I walked towards the garage. I reached my van and put my bags inside. It was either now, or never!

Quietly, I turned the knob of the kitchen door and pushed it open. CRUNCH! My feet stepped and crushed on spilled cereal. There was also milk on the floor and all the breakfast and dinner dishes on every square inch of the kitchen counters. My impulse was to straighten it up. *Don't!* I heard my thoughts shout. *Don't pick up! Don't clean up or straighten up...you don't have time! Get the kids, get some things...you only have eight minutes. Hurry!*

My thoughts kept me on my feet and coached me through the steps I had to take. *Keep the kitchen door opened and get your things!* I did as I was prompted. I quickly grabbed a cooler and quietly threw in some milk, cheese, bread, cereal, chips, peanut butter, and jelly. I placed the cooler by the opened door as the icy air began to pour in to the basement.

I tiptoe raced to my bedroom closet grabbed a few bags and threw in clothes for the boys, the girls, and some for me—hopefully I grabbed enough for a week. I raced into the bathroom and grabbed what we needed. *Hurry! Just run, just run!* I place those bags by the door. Don't forget the Kelpsie (a toy chest for Garrett), the blankets for the kids, sleeping bags...*four minutes left.*

Suddenly I heard someone behind me. Fear gripped my stomach as I turned around. In that turn, I saw my oldest son. My stomach relaxed and I grabbed a quick intake of air. "Mom", he whispered. "What are you doing?" He could see the pillows in my hands. "Where are we going?" With my heart pounding in my throat, "We are going on a little vacation. We were going to take a little trip." He paused. I could see that he was thinking. Then something clicked. His blue eyes locked with mine, and we stared at each other in the dim light. He knew we were leaving. He knew this time we were never coming back.

Through the darkness of the situation, I could see his eyes brightened with hope, and off he ran to grab two stuffed animals. Soon, Isaac followed out the bedroom and also Garrett. They stood there with confused faces, but they never said anything. I told them to quietly put on their coats over their jammies and get in to the van. They did, no questioning, no tantrum, no crying, no hitting; they simply got in to the van. *Three minutes left!*

I then took three trips to put it all in the back of the van as quietly as possible. My head suddenly screamed at me, *Two minutes left!* I ran back inside and opened the door of my girl's room. Urine and foul odors hit me like a wall. I reached in to the bed of my Margaret and lifted up a wet, smelly girl who had a princess dress-up costume on, but the same diaper from school. My eyes were stinging with hot tears; my cheeks were scarlet with hate and anger over the state of neglect I found her in. There wasn't time! I raced her to the van snuggling her face against my chest to muffle her cries. I buckled her in to the van and returned to get Virginia.

I entered back through the dark kitchen door and turned towards the girls' room to grab Virginia. I reached in to her crib and lifted another wet, smelly girl who still had her school clothes on and the same diaper from school. The anger from the neglect of my children was exploding all over my face. I picked up her sleepy exhausted body, held her close so she wouldn't cry, raced her out of the room and buckled her wet sleepy body in to the van.

*Everyone is in the van!* I thought. *ONE minute LEFT!* I turned to enter back in to the basement apartment for the last time of my life. Over the past nine years, I had to return to this basement over three times—never again would I return to this one. For the last time, I would enter the kitchen door, where Thad first lifted me over the threshold. I would pass

the living room fireplace where we had our first Christmas
Eve. I would pass the lights of the Christmas tree. Quietly my
legs flew back to the girl's room I grabbed the final item, the
collapsible crib. I clicked the rails, lifted the bottom, folded
the sides, wrapped it and zipped it in to the bag.

With the crib in my hand, I tiptoed through the cereal
crunched, milk spilled kitchen and in to the garage for the
last time. I left it all behind and shut the door to the basement apartment, never to return. I threw the crib on the top
of everything else in the back of the van and shut the door.
It was packed! It was all here.

I put the van in neutral and slammed my body against
the heavily loaded van. I pushed it out of the garage so that I
would have a clean shot of racing out the driveway. It inched
backward. I pushed again. It inched again. I force the anger
through my push on the last effort and it rolled. With the
momentum, I push the van out the garage and in to the
driveway. My hot breath was going around my head like steam
from a kettle. I opened the door and hopped in to the van and
slammed it shut. My heart was pounding in my chest—breathe!
Breathe! My brain shouted *turn on the engine, leave, run, go!*

I looked down to turn the key—-BANG! BANG! BANG!
Suddenly my father-in-law was there and was pounding on the
hood of the van! He had been waiting. He had been waiting!
He had come through the dark garage—I never saw him! I
startled in my seat with fright letting out a small gasp. "Don't
leave!" he shouted through my closed window. He continued
to pound on the glass. "We can work it out. Don't leave!"

I looked at him and shook my head—I couldn't even speak.
All my words were trapped in my throat. I turned the key
and the engine turned over! I shook my head, I couldn't even
speak! I just kept shaking my head! "NO! NO!" he shouted
banging on the hood and glass window of the van. I pulled
down on the gear shift in to reverse backed away from him.

Then I slammed it in to drive and sped out of the driveway. *Don't look back! Never look back! Get to the main road! DRIVE!* I made it out the driveway and onto the street and turned east. As the wheels spun up the street, I was greeted with clear roads. I turned left onto the highway away from the black dungeon of the basement. I had done as the police officer said to do. I was handed that point of light, and I followed that light through our foggy darkness to our narrow escape! We were out. We had left. We were gone! We had escaped! Escaped to where, I did not know—we were just gone!

# SECTION 6

Survive:
You are the prey,
he is the hunter, and
you don't know where
he is amongst the
foliage and density
of his mind

CHAPTER 28

# Hiding: A Game of Cat and Mouse

H iding. As a child when you play the game of "hide and seek", you (as the one hiding) search for that perfect nook or cranny to hide so that you can win the game. As children, you plan and try out different hiding places. You find your nook and silently wiggle in with just a peephole of vision and you breathe. Without a sound and you wait: Tick, tick, tick, and tick.

You can hear the door creak open and the slamming of running feet are silenced as the seeker begins the search. Bump-thump-bump-thump, you can hear your heart pounding, and you're sure the noise of the pounding will give away your perfect hiding place. The seeker lunges towards the bed, grabs the bed skirt and looks under the bed.... nothing! Your heart skips—phew, safe.

The seeker stands and tips towards the closet, then suddenly at the last moment grasps the handle ripping open the door shouting, "Got You!" Again, the seeker missed! You breathe. Your heartbeats bump-thump, bump-thump, breathe and breathe. The seeker, on their final pass of the room, looks directly towards you. Heartbeats: Bump-thump, Bump-thump, Bump-thump, faster, bump-thump, bump-thump, faster, breathe, breathe…. quiet, you stay frozen wrapped in the curtain, you remind yourself, not a sound.

The seeker scans and scans, raking the room with their eyes, they look one more time in your direction—at the curtain—and then the seeker, disappointed, sulks out of the room. Sweaty, heart pounding, you relax back in to the nook and on your face splits a grin that you are going to win the game! You enjoy the thrill of watching the seeker pass by you because you have outwitted them. However, as an adult, *hiding* because your family's life depends on it, is not the same thrill…. it is not the same game.

I prayed and prayed as I drove through that night to find a perfect hiding place. My prayer never ended. I knew that I had to take my family to where it was safe. I thought about going to a shelter but it wasn't right. I thought about going to my parent's house in Huntsville, but he would find me there. I continued to drive. *Please Lord, Help me! Take me to a place of refuge from this storm. I need help. Please, Please!*

It was late, dark and cold, so cold. Where were we going? What were we going to do? I kept asking myself. I needed to find a safe bed, a warm place. Soon, I found myself driving south, and as I was driving, a light snow began to fall. The snow was soft, it was clean, it was quiet. My thoughts turned towards the idea of Christmas, what were we going to do about that? We had just left our tree and I had just left our whole lives behind us. Well, that would just have to be a later thought—I'll hide that.

I must hide my worry and I must hide my family. My prayers never ceased and I felt guided towards the right place. The right place, the safe place, the nook and cranny to hide was all my mind could think of to find. I would come up with a plan for what to do beyond this night in the morning. For now, hide!

I found myself headed towards a hotel that was close to the school. The direction felt right; that we would be safe for the night. With the snow still falling and lightly sticking to the ground, it started to make a crunching sound under the wheels of my van. I slowed down, turned my blinker on, and pulled into the parking lot. Hide. I must hide the van from Thad if he passes by. After scanning the lot, I decided to park my van in between two large SUV on the southwest side of the parking lot. My van was even part of the hide and seek "game".

I turned off the engine, took a breath to steady myself, and looked around to my children's faces: My three boys were awake, my two girls were asleep, but all were safe. I saw five children ages eight, seven, five, three, and seventeen months of age who were exhausted, confused, but again, we were all safe. My heart uttered another prayer this time of gratitude that we had been directed to know what actions to take since this all began just a few hours earlier. I looked at my oldest son and gave him a smile that I hoped portrayed we are safe!

With the engine off, the cold began to finger its way in to the warmth of the van, so I began the process of unloading the children one by one, but it was cold, that bone-chilling cold. The cold mixed with my exhaustion seemed to intensify its grip on me causing me to start to shiver. Shivering looks like shaking, and shaking looks like your scared, and being scared in front of your children who are feeling so vulnerable at that moment was not a good thing.

I needed to hide my shivering, so I began to move and move. I opened the back door of the van and started unloading our hastily, yet purposefully grabbed belongings onto the snowy ground. My son had thought ahead and had grabbed the cart that was outside the doors of the hotel and pushed it over to me. Together we took the belongings and stacked them on the cart then gathered four of the children around me as I held the youngest and we quietly walked to the door.

I remember holding my youngest daughter in my arms as we walk through the parking lot because she was just wrapped in a thin blanket. She had no shoes or socks on. She still had her old diaper on from daycare. Her feet were red from the cold, and the snow, the light snow was falling on her white innocent face and her little body was shivering from the cold as she rested her body against my chest and shoulder.

The image of her on the night of the escape has burned in to my heart and mind: cold, shoeless, ill-clothed, smelly, wet, hungry. That image gave me a visual representation of the past few years of our lives. It was that of neglect. My baby, my innocent pure baby visually captured the family: cold, home-less, ill clothed, wet, hungry, scared, and exhausted. My heart was stunned by this scene and about the neglect. I had been so busy trying to survive that now this reality of neglect was going to have to be dealt with. I had to hold strong; I would hide that feeling guilt for my neglecting my children, for now.

Going through the door and walking inside the lobby, a gentle wave of warmth surrounded us. There was a low crackling fire in the fireplace. There was a soft warm light from a lamp on a table. There was a warm cinnamon smell comforting us. And finally, there was a tree with soft white twinkling lights, simple decorations, and humble star on top.

Feeling a sense of Christmas, I stopped; my children stopped. We took in the scene of the lobby in with as many of our senses as we could. It was a reminder of Christmas, safety, and love. A reminder of Christmas was right there in front of us not hiding at all. This was a small tender mercy that testified to my heart that the Lord was listening very specifically to my needs and wants. I smiled inside and whis-pered, "thank you."

I turned from the lobby and approached the desk. The clerk looked up from her work and looked at me over her reading glasses with the softest eyes: big—like chocolates. The image of five children dressed in mixed clothing, tired, and haggled mother trying her best to hold it all together gave away our story. She just smiled. Her voice came over us as a gentle hand asking what she could do for us. I looked at her name tag on her shirt, Gloria. I remember thinking that I could shout Gloria and praise God because we had made it to a safe hiding place. Gloria....

I explained to Gloria that we would need a room for three nights. She nodded and began the process of getting us checked in. Small talk was exchanged about the weather, the snow, and the cold as she took care of our needs. Gloria's voice was so soft and so kind. She was another answer to a prayer because she was so kind, so giving, and so helpful. I never felt judged, belittled, or afraid. My children had stayed right by my side as I secured the room, but their eyes and heads were turned towards the lobby, the Christmas lobby, and the feeling of home they had while they looked at it.

After securing the room, I thanked her for being so helpful and kind. I turned with my children in the direction of the elevator and started walking and pushing our belongings. We shuffled forward a few steps when she asked me the question that I'll never forget. "Honey, are you running?" The question stopped me in my tracks, froze me to the spot. My heart skipped, I thought I had been hiding every emotion and circumstance so well. How did she know?

*"Honey, are you running?" The question stopped me in my tracks, froze me to the spot.*

I turned back looked at her directly, ready to give some excuse, but I found myself confirming her questions with a single nod of my head. She just winked at me and held one finger to her lips telling me that she was going to keep that secret. In fact, hide it. I felt relieved. Gloria was going to help us stay hidden. I would have nothing to fear here. I knew that was true. I felt the Lord's love radiate through this angel on our uncharted journey. She left her desk and helped all of us to the elevator and up to our room.

Once everyone and everything was in the room, I reached for Gloria's hand to thank her, and instead, she pulled me in giving me a hug. I leaned into her shoulder and my tension melted and accepted the hug. My mind was quiet. I was quieted with that hug. Then she patted me on the back and looked me in the face took my hand and winked again. I turned took a step glanced and watched her walk down the hall. I turned again, stepped in to the room, and shut the door. I slid the locked in to the case and rested the back of my head on the closed door. We were in, we were hidden, and we were safe—for tonight.

The story might want to end here and be quiet for a while as you ponder about all the events that happened over the past few pages of reading: which were some on the longest, most intense hours of my life. If this story were only about me, I'm sure I would have collapsed onto a bed and cried and prayed and cried myself to sleep. However, with the needs of my children, after hearing the last deadbolt click in to place, I turned to face a room full of five little people who needed a mommy, who needed space, who had sensory needs. Our first night we would not settle in to sleep until I gave them a sense of a bedtime routine. And so, the work began.

My oldest son breathed a sigh of relief, walked over to one of the beds and just fell in to it—boots, coat, and hat on. Asleep. It looked like his needs were met. My second son began arranging his belonging in his ice chest that he calls the "Kelp-sie." He had to make sure that what he had grabbed was right, and he was counting everything and making his stemming clicking sounds as he worked. My third son kicked off his shoes and hopped onto the other bed, and continued to jump and hop and bounce, and jump and jump as he starred as the blank TV. He needed to move, check.

My girls just clung to me. I smelled the neglect on my girls and knew that they needed my love and care. They needed mommy, so the bathing routine began. I started the water, tested it to see if it was warm enough but not too hot, and began peeling off the layers of physical neglect: sticky jelly smeared shirt, wet pants from an old diaper, the princess dress, and the old dead diaper. I hid my exhaustion with a little teasing, smiling, and reassuring them that they would be fine because of my touch.

My love, a mother's love, no one else can care for my children like I do. I placed them gently in the warm water and with fresh soap, shampoo, and a scrub with a fresh cloth, I washed and cared for their needs. I washed away the physical neglect of that night and watched it slip down the drain. With clean bodies, clean hair, clean teeth, clean jammies, and a smell of freshness, I embraced them with more hugs and squeezes. I made a bottle for my baby and tucked in my three-year-old with a real quick story to share for all.

It was time for hugs, loves, and tuck-ins. Isaac's jumping had slowly stopped, and Garrett's counting had finally stopped. I settled the boys and finally, I gently laid my youngest into her portable crib and took inventory of where they all were sleeping. My love, no one else can do it like me. I reassured them that we were all safe. I then dropped to the edge of the bed and said a family prayer. It was basic, short and simple. Once I had delivered those words, I laid at the edge of the bed and pulled a slice of the bedspread over me.

I glanced at the clock, 11:34 pm. I just laid in the dark and silently took steady breaths until the images began to blur and fade into the background of my mind and the blessing of exhausting overtook me. What had I learned? I needed to listen to the Spirit and stay in tune to keep hidden and safe. The caged animal was now changing since we were no longer there. We started to become hunted. Yet, the light even though it had been a pinpoint, had led us through the dark fog to safety. It is over. We were safe...for now.

## CHAPTER 29

# Protection: Finding Safety in the Harbor

Protection: to keep safe; to construct barriers that prevent someone or something from suffering harm or injury; a legal or other formal measure intended to preserve civil liberties and rights. This was my job now—to protect my children. I had not done a very good job of it before. In trying to save our marriage and the idea of having a family, I had allowed a lot of damage to happen. I was going to have to repair that damage that had happened to my family. I was going to protect my children from any further harm that Thad could inflict upon them.

Wednesday morning, about five hours after leaving my marriage and my belongings, I found myself in between the state of dream and being awake. I was very disoriented and in a numbing and fearful fog. Where was I? Had all of what had happened truly come to pass? Or, was this a dream? With that thought of "it had all been a dream", I shot awake! Wake up!

That thought bolted me straight up from my sleep. I looked at the clock 4:32am. I looked around the dark room and could only see the silhouettes of my sleeping children and hear their soft breathing. They were safely asleep. We were at the hotel. We were still safe.

I slipped off the bed and grabbed my shoes and slipped them on. Next, I grabbed my phone from the charger, and the key to my room. I silently slipped passed my children unlocked the door with a heavy click; I quickly assessed the damage that that noise had made…. nothing, they were still sleeping—phew! I walked out to the hallway and closed the door behind me click! I stood frozen for a few seconds listening for any signs of children waking up, and then walked to the end of the hallway with my eyes visually locked onto the door of our room to call my mom and dad.

The thought that had filled my mind over and over was "What was I going to say to them? How, where, or what part of the story do I begin? "Hey Mom and Dad, how are you doing? I'm great! By the way, Thad was arrested yesterday, so I left him—my marriage, my belongings—everything. He was dangerous, and so we were on the run!" Did I say it like that? Well, I almost did.

My parents were long-haul truck drivers. They had a trucking run driving to Atlanta, GA once a week. It took about five days to make the run. They would leave Monday morning about 5:00am, drive to Atlanta by Wednesday, make the drop and pick up the load, and return Friday about 5:00pm. I remembered that it was Wednesday, so they would be the farthest point of their trip which gave my parents another two days of the driving and thinking before they could return home. This was the perfect day to tell them because my parents would need time for it to sink in without being able to act on anything.

My conversation with my parents was so weird. The other phone calls I had made the day before to the protection agency, my sister-in-law, and the bishop, were not as weird. Those calls were because we were in harm's ways, and in need of protection. However, this call to my parents was going to sound so strange to my own mind as I would speak the words.

My parents had saved me so many times, that this time, they were not going to be able to do that—I was going to have to find safety on my own. I still needed love, but I needed to provide the protection. My phone call was a combination of amped excitement, embarrassment, shame, and fear because of the fight or flight response I was having towards the situation. I wanted to sound confident so my parents wouldn't completely freak out.

I dialed up the number. My dad answered. The conversation was brief and quicker than I had intended. I don't remember the play by play of what I said, but when I said that I had left Thad because we were in physical danger, he was quiet. This surprised me. My dad usually has something to say. Through his silence, I could hear my mom asking to speak to me, so my dad handed the phone to her. I shared the same news with her.

Her response was more like I thought; upset with worry, concern, and she started firing off solutions. That must have jumpstarted my dad and he began to join in. One of the solutions that they both fired off was to go to their home in Huntsville and just stay there again. I knew there were going to say that. It was the obvious solution: free-living, full basement apartment, and they were gone all week trucking. However, I told them that that would be one of the first places Thad would look for me, and it would be a three-hour commute round trip so that option was out.

I then felt prompted to tell them to please call the immediate family, my brother and sisters, and tell them what happened. My siblings needed to know what was happening, but I didn't have the time to talk. If I would have called them, they might start firing off solutions or ask too many questions that I didn't have answers to at this time—again this is not a bad thing. However, I needed to say as little as possible, just in case Thad was to call them and try to get information out of them.

My mom wanted to talk longer and to start firing off more questions, but I had to cut her off. I remember telling them over and over again that I loved them, but I couldn't talk any more. I didn't want to stay on the phone much longer because the kids were sleeping, and I didn't want to try to answer questions that I didn't have answers to—it would feel like I had no plan—even though that was true. Again, I told them I loved them and that I would keep them informed about all I was doing. Then, the call was over.

I quickly walked back to the room, slid in the key, watched the flash of green appear, then tipped toed into the room, and rested on the bed until it was time to get up and start the day. I started formulating a day-to-day plan for what we would do while we stayed here. I knew that I wanted to keep the kids distracted from the reality of the danger we were in and instead make it really feel like it was a trip. We were really enjoying this beautiful hotel. I planned on swimming every evening. We planned on how to fix lunches and dinner out of a cooler, and yet still make life livable and fun.

The hotel had a free breakfast, so around 6:30 am, I went downstairs to the lobby and started piling up different cereals, toast, butter, jelly, oranges and hard-boiled eggs onto a tray and took it back in the room were sleepy children were starting to wake up. Soon they were consuming breakfast. They were very excited about all the cereal options—they were actually squealing things like, "Lucky Charms! Fruit Loops! Mom—this is like real cereal!"

Soon, breakfast was over, children were dressed, lunches were packed, and we were ready to leave for the day. The children huddled around me as we walked to the elevator, through the lobby, and out to the van. Soon we were on our way to daycare, school, and work. We started this Wednesday morning like any other work or school day.

Tuesday, yesterday, even though it was only 12 hours ago, felt more like 12 days ago, but it was only Wednesday so I had to plow on to the weekend. A few of my coworkers, throughout the workday, had been looking for a time to talk to me. They all had questions about yesterday and what happened, but I just gave them the look that said, "I'm not ready to talk." Many respected that and had reflected a look back to me; "just know that we are here for you when you are ready."

It was odd. Just the day before, Tuesday at 3:52 pm, I had left a voice message with *Safe Harbor* telling them that my husband had been arrested on charges of assault and that we were in need of obtaining a protective order as soon as possible. In saying words like that, there was a small part of me that just couldn't believe that words like this had even had to leave my mouth. The message committed me to make sure that it was finally, final. Over, finished, done. I had delivered a life-changing message after the office had closed! I had just put my trust in that message that *Safe Harbor* would contact me at some point and help me with the next process. I didn't know what or when that would be, so I just kept my phone close to me and waited to hear throughout the day as I taught school.

The thought that kept going over and over again like a broken record was, "I don't understand how to do *all of this*." The phrase, *all of this* was the following: 1) how to obtain a protective order, 2) find an apartment, and 3) eventually get my divorce. Before all of the events of Sunday and Tuesday, I didn't even know that a protective order was a real thing (I thought it was just made up Hollywood stuff). I have heard about people going to court, filling out tons of the paperwork, and finally obtaining a divorce. However, it sent my head in to a spin trying to figure out if I would understand the conversation on the other end of the phone line about the protective order whenever that was going to happen.

I checked my phone during recess and at lunch—no message, no call. The Wednesday school/work day was beginning to blur past me! Soon, carpool was upon us again, and the school day was over. I collected my children and brought them to my classroom to assess the day, clean up the room, try to prepare for Thursday and wait for that phone call.

Suddenly, my phone began to ring! It was Safe Harbor. I remember two feelings I had: 1) I knew that they were there to help me navigate through this process of obtaining a protective order, and 2) the complexities of the terms, and the court systems were going to be a part of my life for the next few months and even years—this was feeling a little overwhelming.

Honestly, I had never even seen a TV police drama—I had never heard of these terms protective order, filing in court, and the paperwork, until the police officer had told me about them. I had an idea in my head, but when I was leaving the message on Tuesday, I felt like I didn't even know if I was describing what had happened correctly. Words like *assault, violence, arrest, protection order, going to court, petitioner, respondent, being served,* were just so unfamiliar to me I felt embarrassed to use them because I didn't

> *Words like assault, violence, arrest, protection order, going to court, petitioner, respondent, being served, were just so unfamiliar to me I felt embarrassed to use them because I didn't understand them.*

understand them. These things were not a part of my life or anyone's lives that I knew.

The process had so many steps and rules: 1) understand what a protective order was, 2) who can obtain a protective order, 3) how to request a protective order, 4) what was the difference between a temporary order and a final order, 5) how to change a protective order, and 6) what to do if Thad violated the order. Again, terms like petitioner and respondent started to swim around in my head and I would try to replace those words with my name and Thad's name so that I wouldn't be so confused.

I knew the people at *Safe Harbor* were going to be there for me and help me navigate everything. My job at this point was to keep track of the information and to not shut down/shut off my brain when they were explaining to me the steps that I needed to take. The phone call continued and I prayed for strength to not shut down as she began telling me the step-by-step process of obtaining the protective order. I had to trust that the Lord was going to prompt me, remind me, and help me get through this long process.

I learned that first I had taken the right step in protecting my children. I had stepped towards great light through this foggy darkness and found that the light was guiding me from Safe Harbor. That felt great!

After hanging up the phone with them, all I could do was gather my children, drive to the daycare to pick up my girls and drive to the hotel. We had survived another day. It felt like I was no longer in the fog of a night, but that the fog was lifting and that I could see little points of light adding altogether a beam of light to follow. Soon, I would be filling out paperwork for a protective order and we could be safe on a more permanent basis. I sighed then took in a deep breath. This day was done, and we were focused on a stronger light.

# CHAPTER 30

## The Seeker: Searching for Safety

"He came looking for you. He had a photo," Gloria said. This was the news I heard upon entering the hotel Thursday evening. Gloria took my hand and looked at me. She waited until she had my full attention and then she continued. She informed me that someone fitting my husband's description had come into the hotel and was asking too many questions. I was frozen. I just stopped.... this was our first place of safety. This place was our answer, but this answer was not a long-term solution.

I felt like I was suddenly in a time warp where the world was put on pause while in my mind's eye I suddenly saw four to five events happening at the same time: 1) us leaving, 2) us staying, 3) us finding a new place, and 4) us getting caught. I know it took a fraction of a second, but in that pause, I realized that living hour by hour was not going to keep us safe.

Gloria jolted me back to reality by patting and squeezing my hand while looking in to my eyes and said, "You need a plan." There it was, the word I needed, "plan." I looked back in to her soft chocolate eyes and knew she was right. Those two short sentences started to unravel the thin safety net of our

> Gloria jolted me back to reality by patting and squeezing my hand while looking in to my eyes and said, "You need a plan."

hiding place. The game of "hide and seek" was still on. The seeker was still searching for us. This place, our home for three days, was no longer a safe place to hide. It felt like the darkness was starting to creep back in.

This temporary place, our first hiding place, gave us a sense of safety, of routine, stability, and a sense of peace. Gloria, she would nod to us as we came in, and there was a small treat for the kids each night. She helped to keep our secret. We stayed at the school until past 6:00 pm every evening. We would take different routes to the daycare, to the school/work, and back to the hotel. We would eat our sandwiches, cold cereal, and goldfish crackers for dinner. Then we would play at the pool through the evening. But suddenly, it was time to hide again.

I walked quickly to the elevator with my children, as my mind began to race. Hide! Time to hide again. I felt like I was being chased by Thad and by time. So much had transpired over the past few hours and days that I didn't even have time to let my siblings know what was happening. They had no idea that I had even left my husband and was on the run. Now, I was going to need to leave again and find a new hiding place.

As the elevator climbed, my mind raced with the images of Tuesday, November 28th, 2006: 1) the hate and anger of my husband's eyes on the day he was charged and arrested for assault. 2) The look of confusion, grief, and pain of my father-in-law's face when pressing the charges on his son for the assault. 3) The worry and fear of my friend's faces as I told them the story. 4) The fear on the faces of my children. The events of that day were too much, all so fast, and now it was like a checklist. All that had transpired over those past seven hours felt more like seven days. In one afternoon, our world had altered and changed 180 degrees. Ding, the elevator doors opened, we filed out and walked faster to the room.

The key: slide, click, shut, lock, and breathe, pray. Pray: all day every spare minute of the day, throughout the day, throughout the morning, the evening, the night. I never dared to say amen because I felt like I would lose my lifeline, my connection to the Spirit, and my ability to lead and guide this family. Through my constant prayers, the Lord was well aware of all of our needs. My daily prayer was to stay hidden from him so that we could remain safe, and for three days, that prayer had been answered.

That night after our sandwich and cracker dinner, we went to the pool. Since this was going to be out last time at the pool, I tried to make a good memory of it. I remember playing games with the kids. Playing in both pools, carrying, tossing, hugging, just really playing and playing with the kids. Giggles and the magical laughter that my children had echoed happily off the tile walls of the indoor pool and more snow fell outside. For that moment in time, we were free, we were happy. No one was hurting us. We splashed, we played, and we felt joy. I never wanted to see it end. But soon the laughter faded, and the giggles were further spread apart. It was time to wrap up and head back to the room.

We completed our evening routine: bathing, teeth brushing, reading, night vitamins, hugs, and prayers. My precious children were tucked in bed. They still had soft smiles on their faces, and soon sleep would overtake them. My prayer that night was that they would draw from the feeling of that night to help them carry on during the next unpredictable time ahead of us. That dark fog was still surrounding us, but yet, we still had a light to focus on.

CHAPTER 31

# The Plan: Moving out of the Moment and in to the Future!

Plan. It is a simple four-letter word that can clarify and give direction to your life. What was my plan? It had been three days since we ran, and I didn't know what was going to happen this Friday afternoon, let alone for the next week. I needed to review what I DID know: 1) today was Friday, 2) tomorrow would be the weekend, and 3) I would need to find a place to stay. Since I knew that Thad was searching for us, we needed to find a new place. Up to this point, I had been living hour by hour. Just two days ago I told my parents what I could but not all because I did not have any answers for them; I still didn't have a firm plan. Now, it hit me: *Make the plan!*

I woke up, got the kids ready, we ate, and this time after breakfast, we packed up. The kids all knew that packing up meant we needed to leave and go somewhere else; thankfully not too many tantrums or worries. I made a last and final sweep of the room making sure that we had our precious little belongings, and we walked out the door in to the hallway hearing the metal click of the door the last time.

We held on to all our things and walked to the elevator. As the doors shut to the fourth floor and then reopened to the lobby we all saw the tree. That was the reminder that it was Christmas time. That was a bit of a stinging reminder of our loss, but we march through the lobby anyway.

Gloria looked up from the desk, saw us with our belongings and knew that it was time. She helped us checked out. I paid my balance and she held and patted my hand. She looked at me again with those soft brown eyes that were full of love and wished us love and luck. I thanked her with my full heart and gathered everyone and walked out the door never to return.

Gloria was a supporter.

The rush of the morning was upon us and that was the focus. However, the plan was still running different scenarios in my head as we went through traffic, daycare, rush, rush, and rush to school. Phew.... we made it on time again to the school. At school, my mind continued to work on ideas, plans, and ways to remain safe and hidden.

At recess, I was watching the children run, climb, and swing. My head was scrambling to figure out how to teach my next subject lesson when a thought came to mind. *Find out about an apartment.* I told my coworker, my paraprofessional, that I was going to go off campus to grab my lunch.

When lunch came, I grabbed my purse and keys and ran to my van. I had 29 minutes to get this done. The thought that had come to my mind was to get an apartment. Now I know that is not an earth shattering thought, but for me it was. It meant I was looking beyond this weekend of what was I going to do. It meant that I was going to plan at least a month ahead of time. I went to the new building complex that was near our school. I had never lived in an apartment before and I had NO idea how to do this, but I followed the prompting and got started.

To my innocence and ignorance, I had no idea that I would have to wait for an apartment to become available, check my credit score, could only have X amount of people living in there, or that I would have to put money down, or anything like that in order to obtain an apartment. I felt my face flush red with embarrassment, emotion, anger, and stupidity as I was speaking with the apartment manager.

I really thought that an apartment would just be there and I could move in over the weekend. I had NO idea what it all took to get an apartment. However, the manager was very nice. She really tried to make me feel comfortable and helpful. I put my name on the waiting list since that was all I could do at that time, but she promised to call me if something happened earlier. I was late getting back to class, but I just kept up the teaching all the same.

Soon the day was finished and everyone was ready for the weekend. I knew I was. As I was cleaning up the classroom I thanked my paraprofessional again for her help today. She smiled and kept helping. *Tell her.* My heart skipped a beat. The prompting came again; *tell her.* Now—I thought? But, I protested to myself, I had kept everything as normal as possible. What and how should I tell her? I could tell her sarcastically that I was living hour by hour and it was working great? No, I wouldn't do that. I did not want to hinder anyone else with our plight. I did not want to have anyone else be drug in to this situation, but we had nowhere to go; the end of school was coming, and we needed help. The third time the prompting came, *Tell her.*

I took a huge deep breath in and let out a defeated sigh. I screwed up my courage and took a risk. I told my paraprofessional about what had happened to us. It was the strangest conversation. I was watching her face as I explained what had happened from Sunday night to Tuesday and from Tuesday to Friday. The shock, fear, and anger showed on her face. Anger? That last look of emotion was a little confusing to me. She said she was angry with me for not saying or asking for help with anything earlier.

She grabbed me and pulled me in close and just hugged me. I was caught off guard and just stood there stiff as a pole. She pulled back and looked at me and said something I will never forget, "You need help! Stop denying blessings to others! Let us help you." I had no response. I couldn't even imagine what look I must have had on my face in response to this statement, but she ignored it. She pulled me back in and hugged me again. This time I allowed myself to fall into the hug and accepted it.

My mind was racing to try to find an answer to why I hadn't really asked others for help, and all I could come up with was that I was just trying to live hour by hour for my family. I was not thinking about anyone else except for them. She released her hug of me and again, looked me straight in the face. The next words that came out of her mouth were not what I was expecting. Right then and there, she offered for us to live in her basement for two weeks. This weekend was perfect because they were going to be out of town, and that we could stay for a full two weeks while I worked on my plan. I looked at her with wet eyes and accepted her offer—again, another supporter!

That night, I did not drive north to the hotel. My children were nervous, but they trusted me. I promised them that we would go someplace safe, not to worry. I flipped on the radio and again the Christmas music was our constant and familiar companion as we drove out on the freeway. The snow was falling again, just like it had four nights earlier. I followed the directions and we drove through the Christmas lit neighborhood towards our next hiding place.

We found the house, a little 1950's bungalow 30 minutes' drive from the school. It was lit with Christmas lights, and in the front room, there was a tree. It was cute, warm, and inviting. This was going to work for a week or two, and this time I would not wait hour by hour, but I would come up with a plan.

We went to the side door I put the key in to the door, turned the lock, and we walked in. Everyone was holding a bag and their pillow. We were refugees in a new house. It was Friday, the day that signals the weekend, and my children with all of the weeks' worth of stress had finally hit a tipping point. The change from our basement home, to a hotel to now a new basement place to live was too much for them. The inconsistency and instability were pounding on my children, ramping up the emotional volcano that was going to happen.

*The inconsistency and instability were pounding on my children, ramping up the emotional volcano that was going to happen.*

Autism and change was like playing hide and seek through a minefield. As a parent, I would map out a route for the activity and follow the rules, but sometimes even with all the planning and consistency, the kids would step on an emotional landmine. Tonight, as I shut the door behind me and walked down the steps in to the basement, it was all going to blow up! I did my best to support and help them. I usually did my best to prepare them for change, but this week it was just not possible.

This first night in our new place the meltdown of nuclear proportions happened. Garrett was set off by something small, but he had had enough! He bit me, he bit his sister, and started self-injurious behaviors. I had to give deep pressure for him to stop hurting himself and I finally had to place him in a seat away.

My other children started fighting with each other. They were so angry and hurt and it was all coming out at this moment. I just let their emotions all happen. They needed to release the pain and anger some way and so it just kept spilling and yelling all over the place. We all needed that release! After about 30 minutes, I had to come up with a plan and a distraction. While the emotional vomiting was happening, I began searching for anything on TV—nothing, I was looking for books, nothing, then I found a cartoon movie in the DVD player and turned it on. They were all literally screaming and crying and suddenly the music turned on and they stopped! They all just stopped! The distraction had worked.

I let out a huge sigh of relief and went upstairs to cook some spaghetti. This would be our first warm meal in four days and I knew this was something that everyone would eat. As I was cooking upstairs, and the movie was going on downstairs, my mind started planning.

At first, my thoughts started out with the apartment, and the possibilities that I could obtain it in one month, which was the reality, so what would I do for the month of December? I had about ten days I could stay here. I had to meet with Safe Harbor next week to start the temporary protective order. I needed to make it to three more Tuesday classes then it would be Christmas break. Plan "J" would be my parent's home in Huntsville. That would be the last possibility. I needed to find a place to stay for the next 20 days...what could I do?

I was cooking and praying/pondering about how to get to the apartment sooner. My name was on the waiting list, The Lord knew our plight, and I was just going to have to believe that it was going to work out. There were so many moving components with this apartment, and with getting the protective order, and working full time, that I was not going to find any more answers to this part of my plan—so I was just going to leave this piece up to faith.

In finding that answer, I switched gears to thinking long term. I gave myself permission to think that I was able to obtain the apartment. I knew that I was going to get an apartment at least by January, so my next thought went back to my parents. I knew that the Huntsville house was not the answer, but this feeling of living with my parents was something that I couldn't shake. I asked more questions as I pondered the thought of all of us living together again. What I was really doing was brainstorming ideas when suddenly I was prompted by a thought that was long term, even a real answer. I could ask my parents if they would sell their home in Huntsville, and we could build a home together close to the school.

All around my school were new homes being built. This would mean for my parents to move again, sell their beautiful home, and figure out a way to live all together. My children needed stability, I needed support, and my parents could still drive. If we lived closer to the school, then they would be closer to work. I wouldn't have a commute, and we could make a fresh start with new neighbors. It would be a fresh start! The more I thought about it, the more excited I became.

*That was the plan!* I could feel that this was right, but how do I tell my parents? My mom and dad had been trying to sell their home in Huntsville for five months and the market was just dead. They would drive all week, have one and a half days in their dream home, to just pack up the truck and head out again. They never really got to enjoy it or develop roots there. My mom was ready for a change and ready for a way to help us, but it needed to be in a different place.

This prompting was so exciting to me that I felt completely empowered again that I was thinking more long-term, versus hour by hour. This was a good plan in my mind; living with my parents in a new city, in a home we could build, and really starting a new life together. I would call my parents following dinner.

Soon the dinner was ready and we all ate together. It was great to be at a table altogether and enjoying hot cooked food. They lapped up the spaghetti. I watch them gain energy from their full bellies. Once dinner was over, the nightly routine started again, and soon I had everyone settled down in their beds for sleep. It was time to make the call to my parents.

I turned my phone on and instantly I had notices, dings, and bell tones from all the text and voice messages that my family and friends had left me. I knew that I would need to go through all of those, but right now it was time to tell my parents about the plan. I dialed up the number; my dad answered. This conversation was different yet similar to the one three days before. I made it fast and direct to the point: Hi, I'm safe, we are in a new place for two weeks, I have my name on a waiting list for an apartment, I have a long-term plan that involves you both—would you like to know it?

I blurted out the plan. On the other end, there was silence, again. I could also feel that thinking was happening on the other end. My parents said that they would take Saturday to figure some things out and get back to me. I hung up the phone feeling that that was the right response. Now it was time to get to my master's work.

I tiptoed back down the stairs and looked at the sleeping silhouettes of my children. It was good to see them asleep and feeling peaceful. I turned and walked towards the desk to the computer that my friend had and turned it on. I looked at the clock, 9:00 pm, I started my master's work for the week. I had two papers to write based off articles that were due on Tuesday. I needed to get focused and with everyone asleep and tummies full, I started the work.

In my deep focus of the work, and my plan going on in the back of my head, time flew and soon it was past midnight. I knew that tomorrow I could sleep in a bit. That thought was comforting and so relaxing. It was Saturday and I felt like I was going to make this work out. I saved my work, turned off the computer, and fell quickly asleep in my sleeping bag.

Around one in the morning (only about after an hour of sleep) I heard my baby girl wake up. Her cries were feeling out towards me in the dark for help. I opened the small bedroom door, reached in to the crib, and I took her in my arms. I bounced and rocked and soothed her back to sleep. I kept the rhythm going until her dreams overtook her again. I was in a sleepy state as well, and I began to look around on the floor and I noticed that Garrett was gone.

I gently and quickly put my daughter in to her bed and I quietly skirted upstairs to try and find him. Garrett had run away from me before and with the emotional roller coaster, this could be the night that he decided that he needed a break. I check the kitchen side door, locked. I turn on the porch light. Fresh snow—no tracks—phew...he must be in the house. I turned from the door and tiptoed through the kitchen in to the upstairs living room. As I turned the corner, he was laying under the Christmas tree. The sparkling lights encased him in the light as he lay beneath the tree spinning the ornaments and hitting his stomach and making his hissing sounds.

I stood there staring at this scene of a little seven-year-old boy lying under a beautifully decorated tree finding peace and joy. He was spinning the ornaments over and over. I just watch him with blurred vision. My baby, my first grader, my little one with so much against him found solace under a tree. I walked towards him and a floorboard creaked; his sweet noises instantly stopped and I froze. Then he gently started them up again, so I continued towards him. I dipped down beside him to find several candy cane wrappers beside him. I just smiled. What else was there to do at 1:30 am?

I laid with him under the tree letting the light envelope us for quite some time. I was thinking and praying about how the family was going to have Christmas this year. I reached over and hugged him. He kissed my hand and made his soft clicking noise. I smiled at him through shining eyes and the soft light of the tree. He turned to me and said, "Are we a tree to have?" The look in his eyes was so hopeful, so childlike, and so innocent that it sent a small pinprick to my heart. I did not understand how it was going to work, but I felt that it could. I smiled back with my best "happy face" and nodded, yes. With that, he turned and looked up through the branches of the tree, the lights, and the decorations and sighed. I could see the lights reflecting in his eyes and he had found hope. For Garrett, all of this would be over as long as we could have a tree.

I carried him back downstairs and with each step, that small emotional pinprick to my heart started opening up more and more for my emotions to slowly spill out and leak down my face. I tucked him in and reassured him that we were all safe. The opening of my heart continued and I soon found myself shaking with silent sobs on my sleeping bag. I allowed the flow of emotion to rack my body, and I allowed myself to break that night. I cried. I just cried. I needed to release the emotions from Sunday to Friday, and from over the past three years.

Wave after wave of emotion came over me: fear, resentment, anger, and shame. Once shame hit, I was sucked down deep in to the pressure of tears and pain unlike I have not experienced. The depth of inky blackness, the chill and icy feeling, the cold and dark, no light kept washing over me. No hope, just pounding and pounding of shame for not protecting five innocent children. Heavy pressure in my heart started to put weight and constriction on my chest like I was being squeezed in a vice and each turn of the handle put more pain and tightness in each gasp for breath. My fault, my guilt, my shame...completed the final collapse in to the darkness which took me to sleep.

Sleep from exhaustion was never restful. It felt like a wrestling match with an unknown spirit that never let up. Soon, morning light found its way in to the basement. Had hours past? Was it only minutes? Where was I? Again, waking up in a different place was hard.

I grabbed my phone and looked at the time, the date: 8:10 am Saturday, December 2, 2006. The night was over. The morning had begun, and soon we fell in to a routine and we were able to find a rhythm and a structure that worked for us. We stayed in the basement for about ten days. I still attended my master's course, wrote my papers, shopped for food, fed the kids the multi-meal (no one can eat the same foods based on allergies, texture issues and so forth—a story for another time). I also looked for places to live on my lunch break and found time to go to court.

The routine of the next ten days helped me to see that the darkness of my darkest days was fading in to dawn because the degrees of light were increasing signaling that the day would start. With my long-term plan, we would be in more light than darkness, and that was the beginning of real hope.

# CHAPTER 32

# *Safe Harbor: The Iron Strength of Paper*

Survival: Black, inky, tangible darkness thickly enfolded its chilling grasp all about me. I was in a dark abyss. I felt the cold searing wetness of the space, and my eyes scanned for the faintest flicker of light—a pinpoint to grasp onto. Where was I? Was I in a dream in this thick blackness or was this real? My mind could not differentiate the space, darkness, or reality. This chapter is symbolically how I felt while I was at my appointment at Safe Harbor.

*As I sat down in the office at Safe Harbor, my mind's eye was sent in to a flashback of the events that Thad had engulfed us in over the past weeks and I saw the abyss.* I searched and searched for light stretching my eyes in every direction hoping for a pinprick—something in this deep blackness.

My gaze pulsed back and forth hoping for light as I waved the thick watery blackness out of my way. Then suddenly above me, there was the faintest hint of a pinprick of light.

The light waved slightly because I was under deep water gazing up through the rippling surface. *Much like the time I felt my first pinpoint of hope from the police officer when he handed me the card to Safe Harbor.* My gaze honed in on the faint light. The *pinprick* then thickened to become a pinpoint as more and more energy was feeding it. That gentle white thin beam shot towards me through the surface of the wavy blackness. That was it—I reached up towards it!

I focused on that light and push myself towards it—kicking and swimming through the black heaviness that had been holding me back. My hand shot upward out of the blackness breaking the surface and hit the side of something hard—a boat! *The boat in my mind's eye represents the many safe places we escaped to the van, the hotel, and my friend's basement.* I grasped onto the gunnel and heaved myself out of the sucking inky darkness and in to the lifeboat.

With my chest puffing and gasping for air, I suddenly noticed five others kicking their way to the surface. As they broke through the inky blackness they bobbed up and down sending off little ripples all about them. *My mind's eye saw the children were in trauma for years, and they also needed rescue from the psychosis, neglect, and physical abuse from Thad.* I reached over the side of the boat and then lifted and pulled my five children out of the dark water in to the safety of the boat.

Crying and whimpering were coming from my children. I positioned myself in the center of the little lifeboat, wrapping them close to me in an effort to comfort them. I could feel their trembling begin to slow and cease as they relax in to my body. My breathing became more rhythmic, and I was no longer heavily breathing. We clung to each other and my heart sent out of prayer of gratitude that we were safe, it was quiet, and we are floating above the inky abyss.

I scanned across the water to the solid beam of light. It was steady. It was beckoning us to come towards it. *The beam of light represented each day we woke up safe without him!* Our boat was slowly drifting towards the beam. We were headed in the right direction, but we needed to propel ourselves to really get there.

With a deep breath, I knew it was up to me row us towards it. I sat up straight, assessed what we might have in the boat: paddles, an oar, anything? Nothing. I positioned my children safely in the boat, climbed to the bow of the boat, and reached in to the cold black water to paddle. I pushed the water with my cupped hands stroking left hand right hand in an alternating pattern. The boat was slowly going in a forward motion.

Suddenly, a flash of movement caught my eye coming from the inky abyss. With adrenaline laced with fear pumping through me, my arms frantically started splashing, paddling, and rowing through the inky water. *My motion of paddling was carrying us closer to that solid beam of light not only symbolically but in reality, as well. The flash of movement was Thad; he was like a sea monster searching for us. We were still not safe!*

As I paddled through the water, the sky around me gently began to lighten by gentle degrees minute by minute. *My mind's eye thought about that despite the fact that we were homeless, we experienced more and more peaceful mornings because Thad never found us!* Dawn was fighting back the darkness of my past and my eyes had focused on the full beam.

With each stroke, I was closer and closer to making it out of the dark water for good. With morning around me, the light continued to turn upward by more and more degrees, until I saw a clearly defined horizon stretching out in front of me! I finally saw where the beam light was shining from a lighthouse that was towering off a cliff and showing me how far I have to travel across this vast ocean towards land. I plunged forward stroking and stroking till our little boat bumped up on the shore—we made it! *This was how I felt as I put the van in park, took a deep breath, and walked in to Safe Harbor for my appointment to obtain a protective order.*

I walked through the office and sat in a waiting area until my name was called. While I was waiting, thoughts began to fire at me, "Did I look like the faces of these women that were here for help? Is this who I am—battered? Broken? Hopeless? Scared? I realized that, yes; I was a woman in great need. I was a woman who needed to stop wishing for what wasn't, but to deal with what was.

*Suddenly my mind went back to that vision and I saw black inky waves of shame and embarrassment crashing on the shoreline of the harbor.* The waves rising and crashing in a fast rate! *In reality, people at Safe Harbor were walking past me but I did not look directly at anyone. I looked past or through them. I could not look vulnerable!*

More and more waves of black deep guilt for what my children had suffered through—the violence—smashed against the shoreline pounding me with whispered hatred, "you weren't strong enough to admit the truth—your weakness nearly killed your children and you! *CRASH of the guilt wave!* How pathetic, *CRASH!* How can you live with such shame and guilt? *CRASH!*" *The final black wave of hatred and lies smashed against the shoreline of my mind's eye while I physically sat in the office at Safe Harbor.*

As I sat with the advocate and told my story, I showed her each hand drawn picture from my seven-year-old son depicting the detailed angle of Thad's hands grasped about my throat, the barrel of the gun pointed at brother's face, and my crumpled body lying on the laminate flooring with dark shadows all around me, my emotions began to rise.

Symbolically, more emotional waves hit: I began to shake. *The image of the second wave smashed:* my heart was thundering and pounding. *The third waved hit and crashed on the shore trying to suck me back in to the inky blackness* that my trembling became violent shaking. *My mind's eye flashed again to the black water licking at my feet trying to grasp me.* I clutched my arms around my chest in a hug to start to calm me. Suddenly I pulled out of my mind's eye and back to reality: My advocate's warm hands and arms were wrapped around my shoulders holding me. *In that quiet moment, my mind's eye saw the raging black storm lose energy and settle in to still waters.*

Suddenly, her voice shot across the emotion pulling me back to reality when she said the words "protective order." The PO was a court order that barred Thad *like a thick concrete dam* from my place of work, my children's school, my children's daycare, my home, my parent's home, my master's program, places I shopped at and so forth. *The roaring waves were instantly BLOCKED! They were no longer trying to grasp me, pulling back in to the darkness. I was on firm dry land. I was in the beam of the safety of the image of the lighthouse.*

Flash forward from that day at the Safe Harbor office to three days later on Thursday, December 7, 2006. I was in court. I was to obtain the temporary protective order. The court was so fast. I was in front of the judge with my advocate and the judge was reading off something legal and very quick. *My mind flashed back to the imagery—I was on firm dry land. I held onto that beam of light!* That order was good for about 10 days. 10 days free from fear! Thad was not there, but the judge looked at me with warning eyes that Thad would be at court in ten days and to prepare myself for it. I felt my advocate grasp my forearm to help anchor me. *I was within the Safety of Harbor.* I would make it.

I left the court with a copy of the protection order from the clerk's office. My eyes scanned the copy for all the information on it. It was so strange to see my name, *his* name, and a list of all the places where *he* could not see us. Even though it was a few pieces of paper, I felt the strength of it—almost the weight of it. This protection order was like a shield of iron forged and welded together to protect my children, my new family, and me. I felt the weight of it again—the iron strength of paper.

The order stated that I would have five hours to retrieve my belongings without any interference from Thad from the basement apartment in Layton. This was something that I was not prepared to hear. Really? Was I going to be able to retrieve my belongings? I felt a thrill of hope! However, as soon as the hope was in my heart, fear shot through my mind cutting off the hope *like one more cold black wave trying to grasp me.* How was I ever going to return to that basement apartment? My hands started trembling with the thought of it. I could NEVER go back to the basement!

The trauma of entering back in to that basement—in to the smells, the events, the mess, the cereal that was still probably on the floor, the furniture, the food in the pantry...how was *I* going to do it? As I sat in my car, I was so lost in that memory, I was still trembling and I had no one to comfort me, so I bowed my head and clasped my trembling body with folded arms and prayed.

Heavenly Father, I need Thy help! I cannot return to the basement! Help me! Following that desperate prayer, the thought and answer came. It was simple: *Others will be your hands and your feet. Trust others to help you. Others will enter in to the basement for you—freely happily, but you are going to have to trust others to help you.* That thought was so powerful that I stopped trembling and I calmed down. Handing off that huge and important piece to someone else was so freeing! I took deep breaths to calm down and relax.

My eyes continued to scan the protective order. There was another section on the order that stood out to me that stated, "temporary housing." It was filled in on the address line, and it was so strange to read. Temporary housing; it was a huge reminder that we were still homeless and that I needed to figure that out soon. That was my prompt to get going, now! With that reminder, I started my car and began my drive back to work.

As I drove back to school fully expecting to turn in to the parking lot, I suddenly received a phone call from the apartment complex. The manager blurted out that we had been approved and that an apartment would be available for us to move in on December eighth! That was only four days away—on Friday! I held the phone to my head in shock and couldn't speak. I remember my head was moving up and down, but she was not going to be able to see that—-I choked out "thank you!" And then she hit me with a flood of information that was overwhelming, so I asked her if I could come to the apartments right then and meet with her in person. She said that that would be best, so I aimed my van towards the apartments, away from the school, and prayed that my class would keep on going.

I walked in to the manager's office where I was given the information. I put down a deposit and signed the contract for nine months. She then took me to the apartment and gave me a quick tour: It was clean: it had three bedrooms and two baths, and a washer and dryer! As I walked room to room in the 1100 square foot apartment, my mind was racing with figuring out how to set up the home. I could not believe my thousandth miracle and blessing! This was so much faster than I had ever thought possible. My heart was in a constant prayer of gratitude to my Heavenly Father. His *Tender Mercies* were everywhere for me to witness.

I couldn't even believe my other blessing was that I was on the main floor—another *Tender Mercy*. Heavenly Father knew the needs of my children. My kids were noisy. They needed to move their bodies—to jump, to spin, and to rock. With all of my children and all of their challenges, a second floor, or third floor would have cost us our living space because of the noise that they produce. My children run, jump off bunk beds, crash, and were high sensory seekers. What a miracle to be on the main floor!

Soon I found myself back in my van calling my parents to let them know the updates! I ran them off like a checklist: 1) I had a temporary protective order that would last till the hearing on December 15, 2006. 2) I was granted five hours to obtain our belongings from the basement apartment, and 3) I had a place to live and could move in on December 8th! There was relief in their voices. I could feel the thoughts and the wheels turning in my dad's head about all the logistics of how to make this work. My dad and mom agreed that they would pack up the basement for me on Saturday, December 9th and get it in to the apartment that day. I was so relieved and tearful that they could do it all and do it so soon! I thanked them and told them how much I loved them!

My next set of calls were to my Bishop and to friends to see if I could get help in cleaning, packing, and then moving my stuff to my new apartment. The bishop asked what things I needed (furniture wise and food wise) to help me get set up. I was surprised and so humbled by that offer; I didn't know what to really think. I shared my thoughts with him, and explained again and again, how grateful I was for the ward's help. Quickly, I received so many offers to help that I was overwhelmed. I called my parents to tell them that we were going to have support for everything on Saturday, but now, I had to end the call and to get back to school.

I arrived at school just in time to see that carpool had started. It was the perfect timing. I shared my news with my paraprofessional. She actually clapped her hands together and then we hugged. I thanked her for all that she had done to save my family. I thanked her for picking up the load of teaching when I lacked. I thanked her for all her coverage, her care, her concern, and for the basement we live in. She was carrying a HUGE load on her shoulders, and I was forever grateful! I hoped she felt my sincere gratefulness and gratitude for her in that hug. Her smile seemed to tell me that she understood.

I was also able to share the great news with a few of my coworkers. I told them that I was going to have a place to live on Friday. It was a miracle and they agreed. I was suddenly surrounded by a large group hug from coworkers, and I accepted that embrace—it gave me relief and love. It was a great day. Finally, I collected my children, and shared the great news with my kids! We were going to have a home again. We would have a place to be safe and grow again. We even celebrated by getting a pizza even though it wasn't Tuesday night!

The next three days seemed to fly by with the goal set that on Friday we would have an apartment to live in. I was able to attend my master's course on Tuesday, with the help of some lovely supportive volunteers that my friend had contacted. Those lovely volunteers watched my children while I attended my five hours of class. I was able to get through the everyday teaching, loads of laundry, the cooking, the everyday types of living that families need, but none of that mattered. We had a home on Friday! We were going to have a home!

When Friday morning came, I remembered waking early. I needed to clean the basement for my friend. How else could I ever repay her, or thank her? I set to scrubbing the kitchen, the bathroom, and collecting our meager possessions and getting them in to the van. I turned to enter the side door one more time thinking, "tonight, I will have a home again—a place to live, a place we can be safe." Safe; it was such a small word that meant everything to me. I was bound with determination to never go through this homeless experience again. With that

216

thought in mind, I clutched the thank you note I had written with a sense of security. I knew that I would never have to leave a note like this one ever again.

I walked through her dark kitchen and turned in to her living room, to see the softly lit Christmas tree. *There*, I thought, I'll put the thank you note in the Christmas tree. I stuck it in to the limbs of the tree just enough to see the corner but not too much to stick out. I could never fully repay the kindness, love, and support that she had given to us by allowing us to temporarily live in their home for these past seven days. I prayed that she would find the note at the right time so she would understand the feeling of gratitude that I was trying to convey through the words, and then I slowly turned to walk out of the living room never to enter it again.

I went downstairs and I woke up the children, made breakfast, ate, and finally, we were out the door, never to return to sleep here again. Upon shutting the side door of our second temporary home, Garrett turned to me and said, "we have home to go right? We can tree to have?" I actually, smiled at him and could share the answer of yes! We were going to have a tree for Christmas. He turned towards the van, with his feet-shuffling skipping gate, hands flapping, and clicking noise—he was ready. As I watched him walk towards the van, I felt that we were going to make it. I felt that we were on the right track. I felt a few more degrees of light lift my world from dawn to bright sunny morning of my life!

## SECTION 7

# Revive: Restore, regain, start new towards a life of consciousness

# CHAPTER 33

# The Apartment: Safety, Security, and Stability

## First Night:

Once the final student was picked up from carpool, and my classroom was put back in to order for the weekend, I turned and hugged my paraprofessional and thanked her again and again for all of her support. It was surreal to think that just one week ago, she was hugging me and telling me that she needed to serve someone and now we would have a place to live that night. That was a week of love and blessings. We were now going to be able to leave school to a new place to live. I thanked her again, and we parted for the weekend.

Around 4:30 in the afternoon, I slid the metal key in to the door of the apartment and turned it to hear to the doorknob pins fall in to place and the door opened. My children raced in and began running up and down the hallway, in and out of the bedrooms, and in circles in the living space. I turned and locked the door and I smiled. They seemed ok with the place. That was a great sign. After a while, we gathered our small belongings from the van and brought them in to our new home. I sat down on the carpeted floor to make a list of all that I was going to need from my parents. I started with the furniture, then the household items, then finally with the food storage. I was deep in thought when suddenly there came a knock at the door.

My heart leaped up in my throat. My children froze! Who knew where we were? We had only been here an hour at the most. What was going on? I ran to the door and looked through the peephole and again I gasped at what I saw. I dropped down from my tiptoes and with shock a gaping mouth I slowly unlocked and opened the door. There was the most amazing scene that I had ever witnessed: many coworkers and members from the ward had gathered at my door. They had an arm full of boxes, kitchen stuff, some furniture, some bedding, and even a TV/DVD player.

I held opened the door as they marched in carrying gifts of home, treasures of love, a fresh place to start. They brought me a queen size bed, table and chairs, a shower curtain, a few towels, soap, shampoo, laundry soap, pots and pans, some plates, cups, silverware, some kitchen basics, some bedding, pillows, home cooked dinner, and the TV/DVD player with three DVD's! I just sat with my mouth gaping open and my heart overflowing with gratitude. I had no idea that this was going to happen, and all I could do was say thank you, over and over again to everyone who was helping to set up our little home. I looked at the home cooked meal and felt such a relief that I wouldn't have to cook. I hadn't expected anything like this.

At the end of all of their help, they began to gather in the living area and started singing Christmas songs. I felt a surge of warmth and love. My eyes were wet as they sang, and suddenly the apartment door opened to reveal the final surprise: a Christmas tree, decorations, and gifts! They continued to sing, "we wish you a Merry Christmas" as they plugged in the tree and the soft light filled the room with a gentle glow that represented love. I was overcome with joy and my children began dancing in front of the tree and they started to sing again! We were held in the magic of the music, the light, the food, and of love. We were all like kids at Christmas feeling the love and joy of that season. My words of gratitude and my humble heart tried to express my gratitude again and again as they turned to leave. I will never forget the feeling of love, the feeling of gratitude, and the feeling of starting again in our home.

## Moving Day:

The next morning was moving day—it was going to be hard work. My parents and a group of others were going to take five hours and gather our belongings from the basement and bring them here. My job was to stay at the apartment, keep kids busy, coordinate from the phone, and help arrange everything that would be coming to the apartment. My job was easy; my parent's job had to be the most awkward and difficult thing because they would be in my in-law's basement cleaning up, packing up, and clearing out their grandchildren's belongings and sorting through what was Thad's and what was mine.

For me, the packing up of the Layton Basement was something that was going to be very revealing. I could not hide my secrets anymore. The dark secrets of our lives, and of the abuse were going to be on display for my parents and a few good women of my ward to see. It was so embarrassing to have them see the depth of my shame. How I couldn't keep it together enough to even provide the basic needs for my children. I couldn't keep them fed, clothed, or clean. They were all going to see the chaos as I had left it. They were going to see the broken toys, the lack of clothing, and the clothes that needed mending. They were going to see how the seven of us jammed in to a two-bedroom apartment. My secrets were out in the open. I felt very vulnerable at this point, but I knew I had no other option. I again resolved that this was never going to happen again.

My dad had the heavy job: the furniture. He had to move the fridge, and the dining room set from the basement back to their house in Huntsville. It was technically their dining room set: solid oak table, ten chairs, oak credenza, and a huge heavy oak hutch. Then upon returning, he had to move the mattresses, two dressers, two beds, and all the boxes that my mom and two other women boxed up at the house down to the apartment.

My mom and the women of the ward had the worst and more embarrassing job: they would see the apartment and all the "mess" that was left. No one had been in the basement since we left over two weeks ago—and that image of cereal and milk on the floor, dishes piled in the sink, jelly on the countertop, un-vacuumed floors, a dirty bathroom, and clothing chaos (wet sour clothes that had been in the washer for two weeks) was a still image that was burned in to my mind. My mom reported that it was all there. I felt that it reflected on my lack of ability to stay on top of it all while trying to do it all.

However, the work commenced. They boxed photo albums, books, baby books, clothing, some movies, the food storage, my computer, my files, the Christmas decorations (we had set up for Christmas the day after Thanksgiving as was the tradition), the kitchen, our few toys, and then cleaned up the apartment. The rest of the furniture, a set of bunk beds, TV, queen-sized bed, the dressers, kitchen table and chairs, and couch, stayed there. It took the full five hours and a lot of hands, to make the miracle happen.

When they arrived at our apartment with all of the items, my work began. Many stayed to help unpack, set up, unload, and clean. The details are the same for anyone who has moved and set up the house again. But, the feeling of being helped, of being able to manage the overwhelming task in hours, THAT was the miracle. We could have our meager belongings again. We could set up memories. We could be safe and sound in our own home again.

# CHAPTER 34

# Court: Judgments that Protect

"All rise!" the Bailiff's voice rang out loud and clear asking the court to rise, for the judge was entering the court. The scraping of chairs on wooden floors as bodies stood echoed in the chamber. I obediently stood and kept my eyes drilled downward off-centered from the judge's face. As I heard the next command to be seated, my eyes barely lifted from that position. My eyes would reveal feelings and emotions, and I wanted to pull a shade over that—to hide my fear, my shame, my guilt, and my stupidity for allowing the abuse to happen. The judge took his chair, and we were all quietly seated.

"Petitioner, please approach the court." I quietly turned my knees to the side from under the table where they were placed, my feet on the ground walked to the podium with my lawyer, but just back a little and off to the left. My lawyer stood firm and with confidence, I tried to mimic that example, but from where I stood, I was someone who wanted to disappear and become as small as possible. Again, my eyes were fixed just slightly past the gaze of others out of fear of being confronted about my weakness. Outwardly, I did my best to face the judge during court. However inwardly, my mind's eye saw an ugly monster of shame shake its claws and fits at me telling me I was a coward for allowing Thad to hurt my children.

As I stood there in the court, the internal monster of shame wrapped its chords around me making me feel trapped and vulnerable in front of the judge. I felt that the judge was going to look me deep in the eye and scold me for my weakness. I stood there listening to my lawyer read the words I had written that were testifying against Thad: 1) drug abuse. Thad was completely stoned or high, and he would drive with one of our small boys in the truck. 2) Thad would go and pick up drugs at meth houses with my son in the truck. 3) My lawyer read about the special needs of my children who have autism. He argued that I needed to be granted full custody to help the children have consistency, predictability, and routine so they could make progress and ultimately remain safe!

Next, my lawyer read my words that told of that dark, threatening night, *That Night*. After the details were given, my lawyer asked if he could approach the bench. Permission was granted and he handed the judge the drawings from my seven-year-old. He placed his reading glasses on and looked deep at the pictures slowly sliding past each other until he had examined all five scenes. He looked at the shocking drawing of Thad's psychotic episode—his screaming, his *mind friends* that taunted him. He looked over how Thad's hands and arm were up against my neck choking me. The picture told about the gun being pointed at the children, at me, and him.

Finally, my lawyer told of the knife that he held at my throat as I awoken sharply from sleep as he breathed out his last threat that he "was a ninja and would strike at night" because I took away his freedom! The words had truthfully sliced through the silent court and everyone who was in the court heard them.

The judge, my family, the court, they all had heard the story leaving me wide open to their own personal judgments, shock, and retelling, hence my feeling of being vulnerable. A question flooded my mind. Would they look down on me because I didn't take a stand against the abuse until now? It was possible. I would just have to get through this and deal with the pain later. I figured out a way to make it through one more day of humiliation just like I use to make it through one more day of abuse. Like a smoldering ember that turns from dark gray to red hot with flames as the wind blows across it.

When the situation and abuse became overwhelming, I thought I would never be set free because I had picked Thad and I was just going to have to work through it. That thought was my weakness and my weakness was on display. I had taken a huge risk in showing it to a court of law what the children and I had been going through for years. All of that had to be displayed in the court so that I could be awarded the permanent protective order. I was experiencing all of these emotions as I stood to face the judge.

It was now Thad's turn. He had no one to help him. He was alone. He was out in the open and his *mind friends* were on display. When Thad was able to tell his story, it was difficult to watch and to listen to. He kept shifting between extreme calm to extreme outbursts. He would speak like he did when we talked with John (he probably was), then he would shift like he would when he would become Thomas Jefferson. He laughed at the physical abuse accusations. He said it was all a lie. He would laugh and twist his head back and forth.

The judge asked him a question and Thad got very quiet. Then Thad said under his breath that the judge was trying to take away his freedom. He said it again and again. Then he shifted and hunched his back. He glared back at the judge and hissed, "I am trapped! I have no freedom. You don't

understand the control I am under. No one understands."
As those words left his mouth, there was confusion and eerie
silence in the courtroom.

The judge then began looking at the photos of the bruises
of my arms, the marks on my neck, and finally the hand-drawn
sketches of me against the wall with my feet dangling, and
Thad's hands against my neck, the barrel of the shotgun as it
was pointed towards my two sons, and the shotgun pointed
at myself, and finally shotgun as Thad held it to his own
head. The judge looked over everything and was silent for a
long time.

The judge then looked at me, he looked at Thad, and
then back to me. The Judge awarded me the protective order,
and that would be in effect for two years. I would be awarded
full custody of the children. My heart was leaping with hope!
I could feel a smile rising, my lips pulled back exposing my
teeth, my cheek muscles were lifting; suddenly the judge said
that Thad was given one hour once a week *supervised* visitation
to see the children. My cheeks dropped back forcing my lips
to fall back across my teeth and my breath caught. "However,
it would be Thad's responsibility to set up these visits with
DCFS (Division of Child and Family Services)."

I jumped back in my chair with a start as Thad slammed
his hand on the table as the judgment was made. The Judge
pointed his finger at Thad and stated that he was to calm
down. The judge continued on by saying that the divorce
was in the process of being filed so it would not be granted
during this hearing. Thad would be served papers of when
the second court date for divorce would be. The Judge then
lowered his finger, and the gavel dropped down with a small
crack and that was the end of that day in court.

My lawyer prompted me on my back to rise as the judge
walked from the courtroom. I was feeling the sting that Thad
still had a chance to see the children. My feet fell in to a pace
that carried me out of court while my mind was still panicking

over the judgment. The Bailiff pushed open the doors of the chamber allowing me to leave the courtroom first. Once out of the room and in to the tiled hallway, I hugged my mom and dad and gave a handshake to my lawyer as we all proceeded down the long hallway towards the door.

As we approached the exit, I could hear Thad yelling in the hallway. "My freedom! She takes everything!" He became more and more upset. He became more irate. He was yelling and yelling that no one was going to be watching him while he was with his children! Our little group pushed open the glass doors and walked out in to the cloudy December mid-morning and walked away from any more darkening noise.

Once outside, it struck me that I was now legally protected from the chaos, the madness, and the darkness. I was in a bit of a daze and couldn't believe it! It was true what they say about the importance of gaining a perspective. I was finally getting out of a terrible relationship. I was finally being able to feel the difference I felt when I wasn't with Thad. There was a difference. Chaos was all I knew for nearly a decade, it was unfamiliar to have peace, to not have the worry, and to not live in survival mode hour by hour. I had just been granted protection and therefore, freedom to live year to year! This was such a new feeling and I didn't know if I was going to get used to it. I had so much damage to heal from that it was going to take time to heal. I was going to better, but it would take time and take the help of others. It was wonderful to feel less stressed, to be safe, and to be happy!

I was not only getting out of the "forest to see the trees" as it were (although in my case I think my forest was a thick, entangled, overgrown, mess), but I was seeing the bigger picture. Once out of the relationship, I could see the ridiculousness of what it had become, how sick and unhealthy Thad was, and how amazing I felt once away from the chaos. I never was going to go back to that—EVER! I said goodbye to my lawyer and hugged mom and dad again and raced to get back to work, to stability, to my new sense of normal.

With the protective order finalized, my foggy dimly lit days had turned in to a full sunrise of the morning! I was finally free from the dark, choking chaos and entanglement of my marriage. I was able to protect my children with a shield of light of the protective order. I would soon be officially divorced—and then I could really sense peace! Court brought a wave of warm sunshine in to my life and I was finally able to enjoy the warmth of the sun as it filled our days with love and peace.

# CHAPTER 37

## Christmas: Finding Peace

As the eight of us arrived at the church building and put my van into park, I'm suddenly overwhelmed with the images of last Christmas. There was no snow, just cold. It was the kind of cold that keeps you feeling hollow; devoid of light and full of pain. It was the kind of Christmas that you put on an Oscar-winning performance to mask the empty belly, second-hand gifts, and last of the gas to drive to the church so that you can put on the show.

My eyes looked from the odometer, and I released my hand off the wheel. It's time to go in. It's different this year. You have food. You have clothing. You have gas in the van. You have a place to stay. You have gifts for your children. There was hope and light. I suddenly felt a feeling race across my chest and surged upward to my eyes. Tears were on the verge of falling. I took a few deep breaths to keep it under control and from spilling down my face. I kept thinking, I'm here for the Savior. I desire to worship him. I wanted to feel forgiveness for the many years I exposed my children to the abuse.

I wanted the love of my Savior to fill my heart and displace my hurt and my anger so that I would have peace.

With each step on the crunchy icy sidewalk, a voice of doubt raised questions: Would anyone really say hi? Would they point and gossip? Would they forgive us? Would the feelings and judgments that they had against us be forgiven so that we could all worship on Christmas Eve? My final question brought me to the front door where I would learn soon enough if this were the case.

I hurried the children out of the cold and in to the warmth of foyer. We stomped off our icy feet and hang up coats to get settled before walking in to the Chapel. I remember turning from hanging the last coat and I found arms wrapped around me and a whispered "Merry Christmas" in my ear. She released her hug on me and looked at me with swimming eyes and choked out, "welcome home." My heart and face were surprised as I tried to return the smile. Then a second ward member gave me another warm hug. I was surprised by this welcome too, but I relaxed a bit to enjoy the hug, and then pulled back and wished her a Merry Christmas. That was something that caught me off guard. Two hugs from people I was not expecting. Was all of that real?

My children huddled around me like little ducklings and we followed my parents in to the chapel and sat down. We heard many ward members in the gathering congregation giving good wishes, Merry Christmases, and warm greetings to one another. I saw a sea of green, white, and red sweaters, knitted scarves, warm coats, and happy smiles. We found an open pew and slipped in. As I settled the kids with coloring books, I felt a hand on my shoulder and I looked up at the gentle pressure; it was my visiting teacher. I stood and she gave me a hug. Both our eyes were wet with tears. Nothing was said, how could we say anything? The history, the pain, the lies, the excuses I made, they all seemed to melt away. We just stood and smiled and blubbered a bit. Several members came up to me and wished me a Merry Christmas. I found many open arms, warm hugs, kind eyes, and smiles. This was different then I had expected and I allowed myself to envelope myself at the moment. The gentle prelude music filled the chapel with Christmas hymns and the stand was filled with the choir.

As Sacrament Meeting started with the opening hymn, my heart and emotions began to feel a change. My pain, guilt, and shame began to fade from fresh red, hot stinging welts and burns to blisters signaling that the process of forgiveness was beginning. My tears started to flow releasing more pain from guilt and shame. It was as if the newly formed blisters were now rupturing and the new pink skin underneath was beginning to emerge. My heart was healing from the pain of the judgment that had been passed on me about Thad's actions. My heart was forgiving the shame of why I had stayed with the abuse for seven years.

When the Sacrament was passed to me, my tears were flowing out of love for my Savior who understood my pain and took it upon himself in the Garden of Gethsemane. As I partook of the bread and of the water, I could feel the healing hand of forgiveness in my life. I felt that I was being forgiven for exposing my children to so much pain and abuse. I felt I was forgiving my neighbors and fellow church members for judging me as I felt Christ's healing love fill my soul. This love was gentle and powerful, and my eyes could not contain it and it ran and ran down my face.

Following the passing of the Sacrament, the choir took over the rest of the meeting. They sang hymn after hymn of the Savior and his birth of the tiny babe born in a manger. They sang of Mary and of Joseph and of their love for this little child. They sang about the humble circumstances of his birth. They sang of the Angels that foretold the birth, and the Shepherds that witness the tiny Christ child. The violin and piano played for the Christ child; it was all brought forth in the power of music. Then my favorite hymn "Silent Night" was sung with humility, simplicity, and love, as this gentle hymn should. As the last note faded into the air, the silence of that Christmas Eve rang within my heart, I felt the power and joy of Christ's love for me.

Following the closing prayer, we stood to leave, and a gathering of people who wished us Merry Christmas surrounded us. They reached out and hugged us again, we forgave each other, and they wanted to help. They had tears, I had tears, and the hard feelings I had towards anyone had melted away through the gift and love of the Savior. I was healing; I was forgiving others for judging me. I was also being forgiven for judging them. That gift at Christmas was something that no one could have ever wrapped up because it was from the Master Healer Himself. I felt love and healing throughout the meeting; with my neighbors at that moment was very powerful and humbling and a gift I'd treasure forever.

We left the chapel and headed to the foyer to start the ritual of bundling up, boots, hats, and gloves. Once we were bundled up, we found ourselves driving on the icy crunchy roads to my parent's house. As the sun started to dip behind the mountains the cold gripped the valley. We passed homes with families, food, and trees lit with sparkling lights. Home after home of colorful outlines of roofline and eves also welcomed us home. Mile after mile our van crunched along the icy roads until we turned up the gentle slope and in to my parent's neighborhood. We passed the Red House and it too was lit with lights. I saw the tree in the front living room shining through the window. It was nice to see someone enjoying the home the way it was intended.

Our tires crunched to a stop in the driveway and I put it in to park. The afternoon melted into Christmas Eve, and it was time for the tradition to begin. We unloaded my five precious children from my van and quickly got inside my parent's home. Coats, boots, and gloves were shed in the mudroom, and in to the large room we ran! My dad went right to the wood fireplace and stoked up the fire while I helped my mom with the food for dinner. We pulled out trays of food, pies, cookies, rolls, meats, potatoes, veggies, cheese, crackers, and Christmas Jell-O. I had prepared a lot of it the day before so that all we would need to do would be to set it out and enjoy the feast.

We sat at the table with the food in the middle and bowed our heads for a blessing on the food. My dad offered a wonderful prayer and we thanked the Lord for our blessing this day. With a hearty amen, we set in to feasting! I enjoyed mixing the flavors, remembering the traditional foods, and watching my children eat and enjoy themselves.

My dad started playing music on the piano, while I helped the kids clean up from dinner. The cleaning quickly stopped and we left the mess to sing carols. The kids danced in front of the tree. I snapped a few pictures to remember this Christmas, since this was the first one with our different size family. There was no stress, no worry, and I was living in the moment.

Soon my oldest found a gift under the tree and asked if he could open it. All the children were able to open one gift. They ripped through the paper tossing it all around, and with squeals of delight, they all found the matching pajamas that my mother had sewn and sewn through the long weekends of December. They were perfect. Quickly, everyone was dressed and more pictures were taken. We sang a few more songs together and then it was time for bed. It was such a great evening: full tummies, full hearts, and it was full of family.

We hugged and kissed grandma and grandpa goodnight. I held Virginia as the rest of the children followed me downstairs to the bedroom. We had loaded the beds with all the extra blankets we could find. How do you get excited kids into bed? They jumped on the beds until they were burned out of all their energy. We did a more sensory and deep pressures games, then melatonin. Finally, after many more stories, I finally tucked and tickled the kids into their beds. As they became more and more sleepy, I read from Luke chapter 2, the story of Christ's birth.

Soon their eyes were drooping off to sleep. I stayed with them in that little room as the light from my lamp pooled around me. I hummed a few more songs until Virginia had drifted off to sleep in my arms. Peace. I dimmed the lights and the gentle sleep was upon my children. I watched them bathed in the light of the nightlights that I had in the room. I looked at their rising and falling chests and their soft faces. This was peace, this was happiness, and this was Christmas. I knew in the morning that they would be up early ready to open the gifts but for me, this was perfect.

As I shut the door and stepped up the stairs to my room, I thought about the miracle of the day. Step. The safety. Step. The forgiveness. Step. The fun. Step. The kids opening up their gifts. Step. The love we all felt. Step. The peace and love were something that my heart held on to. I knew that I still had hard times ahead, but we were free from Thad. We were free from the fear. We were free to make decisions based on our own lives and not waiting for the "other shoe to drop."

During this cold crisp night, even though the dark at the top of the stairs, I didn't feel darkness. There was only peace and soft warm light from my Savior. My heart opened up in to a prayer of gratitude that we were here, that we were safe, and that my children felt loved. The pinpoints of light that brought me here shone all around us and through us penetrating the darkness until we felt like we were home. For us, the pinpoints light had led us to the full brightness of the day and our days would never be darkened to the depths of blackness ever again.

## EPILOGUE

# Thrive: To prosper and flourish because you are in the light of love

Smooth and shiny, the packing tape passed under my hand as I slid it along the seam of the last cardboard moving box. I sighed. I snapped off the lid of the black sharpie and wrote a description of the contents in the last box. I snapped the cap back on and sat back and read the words: Wedding pictures, wedding book, engagement photos, and pictures of cute new babies. I smiled. My fingers tapped a goodbye to the words written on the box as I gently handed it off to my oldest, my 17-year-old. He turned and walked out the door. That was it; the final box. That last box held so much growth and change since we had moved to the Amberly home September 11, 2007.

My eyes slightly fell out of focus as my mind slipped into the memories of the past eight years. I looked at the freshly painted walls, at their emptiness. I saw the places where my family pictures had hung and smiled down at me. I tucked my knees underneath me and fell on to my back. Right here on this piece of carpet, I remembered the rocking chair as I would hold and rock my babies in this room. They would drift back to sleep in quiet and peace. I glanced over to where the master king size bed used to be and smiled as I thought about the rest, comfort, and the sleep that used to cradle us there.

I stood and walked across the bare room leaving sock prints in the freshly cleaned carpet of my master bedroom. I walked out the door and look around the upstairs open hallway and saw four open doors leading in to four empty bedrooms. I quietly walked to the largest room and smiled as I remember the four different sets of beds that used to line the L shaped room. It started with the three boys living here. Next, we changed it to our master bedroom. Then to the preschool I had, followed by the video studio, and the library. Finally, I had moved my four daughters in to this room.

My eyes fell upon the door to the deck. I open the door and step out to the deck and looked at the west facing view. The view of rooftops, endless sky, and the amazing sunsets from this deck flooded my mind. But it was too hot in the heat of August to reminisce much longer, so I returned to the coolness of the room and shut the door.

I walked back through the door to the open hallway that overlooks the foyer below, and with a firm grip, grabbed onto the railing and tugged it a few times. Solid. I remember the permission we needed to get from the builder to bring an exterior railing in to an interior space. That was a must for my children, my dad said. He was right. My children would hang and climb on nearly any surface they came in contact with, but with this railing, it would hold up under the strain of nine children swinging around the posts as they flew down the stairs.

I turned and looked in to the bathroom. My laughter escaped my mouth as I remembered seeing Garrett perched on the countertop with his head upside down looking at the water running out of the tap, and his right hand drawing the individual droplets of water as it cascaded from the faucet.

My face also dropped as I remembered that sink swallowing my wedding ring that Scott had given me. I took wrenches and pipe cleaners to it and took all the plumbing apart looking for my ring. Hoping beyond all hope that it was stuck in the P-trap, but no luck. I turned from there and looked at the tub. My mind could hear the laughter of my children skipping like sunshine off the surface of the water as each had bathed there. Those sweet faces and my heart melted.

I took a few steps out of the bathroom and walked in to the second bedroom. That room had seen a lot of paint and change as well. It had started off as the playroom, then changed to Kellis's room, and finally to Garrett's room. In the memory of the playroom, I could see my three boys playing with their Legos, and my mind played back the memory of the old computer reading off "Arthur's computer Adventure!" I chuckled a bit to myself as I could also hear the trivial fights between siblings but smiled as I felt the warmth from the love from their bursts of laughter when they would play games together.

I ran my hands along the door casing as I left the room and with a few steps turned in to the third bedroom. As I pushed the door open, I saw the walls change from bubblegum pink with green fairies to neutral brown, to gray. Even though the room was empty, I saw the bunk beds, then the loft beds. I saw the nightlights, the lamps, and the ceiling fan. I remembered the cries of pain from a very sick child with whooping cough. I can't believe that six of nine of our children got sick with whooping cough. That was a long and hard week full of coughing, gasping for breath, medicine, vomit from the coughing, the holding and rocking, the praying for it to end soon. This room was always my hospital room. I think because it was so quiet, and it was small. I felt I could contain it there.

I turned away from the room and passed the laundry room. I smirked and touched the doorframe. The walls and the floor seemed to never stop rattling and humming with the ghost of the black washer and dryer. Those machines never stopped. There was a constant slosh of the washer and rhythmic hum of the dryer as nearly 24 loads of wash per week were done here. It was like running a small hotel. It served our purposes well.

My hands left the casing, and I made my final step towards the last bedroom and peeked in to the bright east facing room. The flood of memories returned, as this had been the place where I had first slept in this house. I recalled my first night in that room: I pulled back the covers, I slid under the sheets, took a deep breath and sighed, I'm home.

Deep in the memory, I was closing my eyes when suddenly the opening and slamming of a door and the pounding of running feet to my bedroom when the door flew open! I saw three little faces come running and jumped on to my bed! It was the boys. They were scared to sleep away from me. I half laughed and half sighed. It was true because for the whole time we lived in the apartment, they had basically been with me in one room. Many nights I would tuck them in to their bunk beds only to find them in my bed in the morning. Sleep had been the priority, and where that sleep took place did not matter to me because sleep just needed to happen.

I turned out of the fourth room, sliding my hand on the smooth surface of the top handrail, around the post and went down the slant of the first seven steps until I reached the landing. I looked to my left at the large 17-foot wall in the foyer. I stepped off the last stair and look at the large canvas of the blank wall, and remembered my wedding photos, my start of a new family. I could see in my mind's eye the faces of my five children as we huddled together on our wedding day. The children are positioned all around my new husband and me at the Bountiful Temple. We were married on April 2, 2009. The pictures captured my new family all together in one place. My smiles, my husband's smiles, and the eager looks on the children's faces were captured in black and white and hung for all to see.

I quietly stepped down the last eight stairs to the bottom step and froze there. I looked at the entire foyer and to the right of where the wedding pictures used to hang. In that spot were the pictures of all my children plus four more children who joined us for a total of nine. Marianne came in 2010, Rhetten, in 2011, April Rose in 2013, and Scott Joseph came in 2014. Marianne and April Rose were born deaf. That quick smile and strong headed girl, Marianne, shaking her fist at the water at a waterpark, and that sweet little Rose of a girl with a smile that melted your heart was the reason for our empty house.

I thought about my first five children and how I had moved heaven and earth so that they could be safe and had the proper education to help them with their autism. I helped to create a school that gave them a foundation that set them up for success. I did everything in my power for them. And now, I was faced with helping two more of my nine children. I closed my eyes and remember the day I learned that Marianne was deaf. I opened them again when I thought about the day I learned that Rosie had autism and was deaf and blew out my breath. I knew that the earlier we gave supports, treatments, and intervention the better her outcomes would be. This move away from all we knew and loved was hard, but it was right to go to Texas and on that faith, Scott and I packed up the family and were headed off to the great unknown.

I stepped off the last step jolting me out of my thoughts and turned to see my husband's music room. I could hear the ring of his guitar as he blasted it through the amplifier. I remember the run of chords, the songs, and the practice. I remember the band members that visited him. I loved the hours of video editing in this office for my curriculum. Those were times Scott and I worked the longest and the closest with each other. Again, I smiled.

I walked a few steps to the right and I came to one of my favorite rooms, the dining room. I entered the hollow sounding room and stood on the spot where we told each one of the children of my engagement to Scott. I remember eight-year-old Garrett running up and landing on his lap asking him if he was going to be a "good husband or a bad husband." Garrett put his face right against his face and stared him hard in the eyes. Scott said, "I'll be the best husband." Garrett pulled his head off his forehead and smiled and jumped off his lap and ran off to play.

My eyes followed the memory of his running legs in to the kitchen/great room combination. I stood still; looking around the kitchen that was so full of memories. They had no beginning or no end. There had been birthdays, grandparents, cousins, uncles, aunts, in-laws, Thanksgiving walk arounds, Christmas breakfasts, fall canning, making grape juice, grape jelly, spaghetti sauce, chili sauce, and apple pie filling. There had been hot summers making ice pops, long nights making bottles, and then the all the short-order cook meals each evening. I taught my children how to cook in this kitchen, and that brought a pang of tears to my heart.

I turned to look in to the empty family room and stared at the wall where the TV hung. I remember watching the many Olympic games, the World Series, the endless cartoons, and the home movies. I looked at the corner of the room where we would set up the Christmas tree and remember the tradition of keeping the kids at the threshold before running in and enjoying the splendor of Christmas.

My eyes then looked at the large picture windows that gave the view of the backyard. I grasped the metal doorknob and pushed through and walked to the back patio. I looked at the southwest corner of the yard and at the American Red Maple that we had planted. I then looked to the Northwest corner of the yard and found the Newtown Pippin Apple tree and Concord Grape Vines that stretched down the north side of the yard. In 2014, those vines gave me my biggest yield of grape juice ever: 43 quarts of juice. I remember that year because I had asked for help in harvesting and canning because I was going to have my last child. Three days later and he came right on time.

I walked the perimeter of the yard looking at the garden boxes that Scott and the boys built. Our tomatoes thrived, our peppers were pumped, but our pumpkins only lasted two years then we were hit with squash bugs! A wave of anger welled up at the thought of those pests destroying the only crop my children loved, pumpkins!

I stepped out on the newly laid paving stones on the south side of the house. The dirt was still fresh in spots where Kellis and I had removed the soil, laid the barrier, the stones, and the pavers. I walked through the gate to the front yard. I turned to look at the petunias in the front flowerbed enjoying the afternoon shade after a hot August day. I took a step in to the shade of the house and looked at the front porch. The welcome sign that always hung a bit crooked, the red, white, green, and yellow painted rocking chair that we enjoyed as we watched the children play in the cool of the evening. It was all gone. It had been packed away.

This had been our home since 2007. My parents and I had built it. For us, building our home was not about the materials, the layout, or the finishes, but it meant that we were really going to have a home. To me, a home meant family. It was a place of refuge from the raging, angry, filthy, and scary world of Domestic Violence. This home was a protection and a barrier from all of that. And finally, it was a place of healing.

In my dark life when I was married to Thad, we built and sold homes over and over again. That was the construction business. I knew what it took to build a home, a living place, and a place to hang your hat. But for me, our home on 1047 Amberly Drive was so much more than that. It was a place where I taught my children the love of Jesus and of His Gospel. Through that teaching, we felt love without the interruption of substance abuse. Our home became a place where we could talk about my children's needs, their wants, and their dreams. It became a place of safety, of refuge, of building trust and love.

At first, it was just my children and parent who enjoyed the home together. Then we added Scott in 2009. We found room for all of us. In 2012 my parents moved one block away to give us space yet close enough for the children to keep their relationship. Together, we enjoyed our Amberly home for three more years. But on that August day in 2015, as I stared at the home, I felt like I was leaving a friend behind. Our home was a faithful, protective friend. It was so hard to leave it. All the investment, the time, the maintenance, but it was sold, and we would pass it onto another family in two weeks.

I walked towards the street and leaned against the sold sign in the yard, my head turned to take in the home one more time. I looked at eves standing straight, the black shutters that matched the black door shining smartly, and the brown-reddish brick that protected the walls from the extreme heat, and extreme cold. I smiled at her, and in my heart, I swore I heard the echoes of children's laughter coming from through the open window from upstairs. I look down the soft grass and my heart smiled at the flood of memories that spilled out of my eyes and gently kissed my tired cheeks. I looked up one last time and saw a pinpoint of light at the tip of the gable as if to say goodbye. "Goodbye", my heart whispered, "Goodbye."

My children and me in spring of 2007 six months after leaving
the abyss of abuse. Garrett (7), Isaac (5), Kelllis (8),
Margaret Susanna (3.5), Virginia Grace (2)

Scott, April, & family Wedding day April 2, 2009

# BE THE BRIGHT LIGHT OF YOUR FUTURE

**Join the Dusk to Dawn Events** to **strengthen** your battered, beaten, and broken self to become a **Victor** in **light** and **life!**

- **Imagine** finding your **individual worth** and shining that worth for others to see.

- **Imagine** the journey of **healing** from the deep darkness of abuse into the **dawn of life** by learning your **self-worth**, your **strength**, your **value**, and your **power!**

- **Imagine** how to **share** your **light**, your **power**, and your **love** with others who are broken to **add** more **light** to cast out darkness and fear.

**Dusk to Dawn** trainings and events are powerful experiences that lead the *battered, beaten, and broken to* discover their **strength** to **heal** so that they become a **victor** in **life** and **light!**

**Participants** can **join** from **anywhere** in the **world**.

# Who is Transformed?

## VICTIMS BECOME VICTORS
## SUPPORTS BECOME VALUED
## ADVOCATES UNDERSTAND
## THEIR IMPACT

*You are worth the transformation from Dusk to Dawn*

FIND OUT MORE WWW.PINPOINTSOFLIGHT.COM

**April T Giauque** is an **author, speaker, coach**, who helps the *battered, beaten, and broken* **discover** their **strength** to **heal** so that they **become a victor** in **light** and **life!**

**Author/Speaker/Coach/Strengthener/Enlightener**

## Bring April to your Organization

April knows the importance of selecting the best speaker for your setting. The speaker sets the tone for learning and enlightenment, which can be transforming or disastrous. Her sincere and energetic delivery to each and every individual in the room is unheard of. April customizes her events to meet and exceed the needs of the client's personal objectives. Her goal is to bring others our of the abyss of abuse and light!

# FROM DUSK TO DAWN

## Why Stay

Love
Finances
Religious Beliefs
Low Self-Worth
Fear
Shame
Isolation

## Steps to Leave

Build a support network
Financial independence
Separate Bank Accounts
Make an escape Plan:
72 hour kit
Know your local
Supports:
police, crisis centers, etc

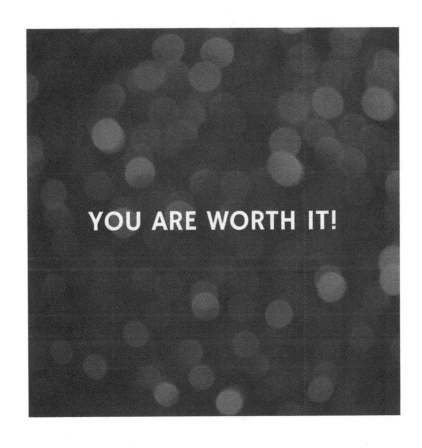

YOU ARE WORTH IT!

9 781640 853515